PERSPECTIVES IN READING

The Evaluation of Children's Reading Achievement

INTERNATIONAL READING ASSOCIATION

PERSPECTIVES IN READING NO. 8

THE EVALUATION OF CHILDREN'S READING ACHIEVEMENT

Compiled and Edited By
THOMAS C. BARRETT

University of Wisconsin

Prepared by a Committee of the
International Reading Association

Thomas C. Barrett
Chairman of the Conference

INTERNATIONAL READING ASSOCIATION
Newark, Delaware 19711

INTERNATIONAL READING ASSOCIATION

OFFICERS
1966 - 1967

President: MILDRED A. DAWSON, Sacramento State College, California

President-elect: H. ALAN ROBINSON, University of Chicago, Illinois

Past President: DOROTHY KENDALL BRACKEN, Southern Methodist University, Dallas, Texas

Executive Secretary-Treasurer: RALPH C. STAIGER, University of Delaware, Newark, Delaware

Assistant Executive Secretary: RONALD W. MITCHELL, International Association, Newark, Delaware

DIRECTORS

Term expiring June 1967
  DOROTHY M. DIETRICH, Union Free School District, Uniondale, Long Island, New York
  HELEN HUUS, University of Pennsylvania, Philadelphia, Pennsylvania
  ROY A. KRESS, Temple University, Philadelphia, Pennsylvania

Term expiring June 1968
  ALTHEA BEERY, Cincinnati Public Schools, Cincinnati, Ohio
  BROTHER LEONARD COURTNEY, FSC, St. Mary's College, Winona, Minnesota
  GRACE MC CLELLAN, Child Guidance Clinic of Greater Winnipeg, Winnipeg, Manitoba

Term expiring June 1969
  MARGARET EARLY, Syracuse University, Syracuse, New York
  THEODORE HARRIS, University of Wisconsin, Madison, Wisconsin
  EVE MALMQUIST, National School for Educational Research, Linköping, Sweden

Publications Coordinator: FAYE R. BRANCA, International Reading Association, Newark, Delaware

Copyright 1967 by the International Reading Association, Inc.
All rights reserved.
Printed in United States of America

FOREWORD

WHEN considering the areas in reading instruction most appropriate for consideration in the 1966-1967 year of IRA, there seemed to be none more deserving of attention in a Perspectives Conference than that of evaluation. With the approval of the IRA Board of Directors, Thomas C. Barrett was invited to plan and implement such a conference in conjunction with the annual convention of the National Council of Teachers of English at Houston. He did a superb job as the readers of this bulletin will testify.

Advisedly the Perspectives Conference opened with an address that explicitly defined what evaluation in reading is, what it does, and when it should be done. In related fashion the next speaker presented the goals of the reading program. The next two speakers discussed informal techniques in assessing prereading behavior and the use of reading readiness tests in prediction and diagnosis. A half dozen speakers then gave a well-rounded look at evaluation after children have been introduced to systematic reading instruction: survey reading achievement tests, diagnostic reading tests, the supplementary but invaluable informal reading inventory, the use of teacher-pupil conferences, evaluation of the affective dimension of reading, and relationships between teachers' questions and the levels of pupils' reading comprehension.

In reading this bulletin, teachers and supervisory-administrative personnel will find aid in gaining a philosophy to guide their programs of evaluation. In addition, they will get help in setting up a thorough and valid program of evaluation in the classroom.

MILDRED A. DAWSON
President, 1966-1967
International Reading Association

CONTENTS

		Page
Foreword		iii

1. Evaluation: What Is It? Who Does It? When Should It Be Done?... 1
   Margaret Ammons

2. Goals of the Reading Program: The Basis for Evaluation...... 13
   Thomas C. Barrett

3. Informal Techniques for the Assessment of Prereading Behavior.. 27
   Dolores Durkin

4. The Use of Reading Readiness Tests for Prediction and Diagnosis: A Critique..................................... 35
   Robert Dykstra

5. The Selection and Use of Survey Reading Achievement Tests.... 53
   William R. Harmer

6. The Values and Limitations of Diagnostic Reading Tests for Evaluation in the Classroom........................... 65
   Wallace Ramsey

7. The Informal Reading Inventory as a Means of Improving Instruction... 79
   Robert A. McCracken

8. Teachers' Questions and Levels of Reading Comprehension.... 97
   Frank J. Guszak

9. Evaluation Through Teacher-Pupil Conferences.............. 111
   Lyman C. Hunt, Jr.

10. Evaluating the Affective Dimension of Reading............. 127
    David W. Darling

MARGARET AMMONS

UNIVERSITY OF WISCONSIN

1. Evaluation: What is it? Who Does It? When Should It Be Done?

BEFORE discussing what evaluation is, it may be helpful to make an assertion regarding current education and the relation of evaluation to it. In the final portion of the paper, this point is raised again.

The assertion states that in today's school there is determinism, i.e., individuals are classified early in their school careers and tend to retain that classification throughout their years of schooling. Evaluation, properly employed, can reduce this determinism.

Analysis of Evaluation

Historically, four classes of activity have been associated with curriculum development: 1) identification and formulation of educational objectives, 2) selection of learning activities, 3) organization of learning activities, and 4) evaluation. By definition these four activities are closely related, mutually dependent. Therefore, in order to discuss evaluation it is necessary to construct a context by defining objectives and activities and describing their relation to each other and to evaluation.

The specific topics which comprise the remainder of this paper, are as follows: 1) definition of terms, 2) characteristics of evaluation contrasted with such activities as testing, 3) identification of techniques, 4) individuals responsible for evaluation, and 5) some recommendations for a total evaluation program.

Definition of Key Terms

As stated earlier, the major activities in curriculum development and improvement focus on objectives, learning activities, and evaluation. For purposes of clarity the following definitions are used throughout the discussion.

Educational objectives are statements of purpose which contain a description of possible and desirable student behavior and an indication of appropriate content. Important at this point is the recognition that behavior, as it is used here, is much more inclusive than those behaviors which are observable. One useful illustration of possible student behaviors can be found in two volumes, *Taxonomy of Educational Objectives—Handbook I: The Cognitive Domain* (*1*) and *Taxonomy of Educational Objectives—Handbook II: The Affective Domain* (*3*). Within the cognitive domain the following behaviors are included: knowledge of specifics, comprehension, and application. The affective domain considers five different behaviors: receiving, responding, valuing organization, and characterization by a value or value concept.

In the case of both the cognitive and affective domains the behaviors are said to be listed in the order of increasing complexity. Thus, knowledge of specifics is the simplest behavior, and evaluation is the most complex. Similarly in the affective domain receiving is the simplest with characterizations being most complex.

In either domain, content is conceived of as much broader than material found in a book. The intent of the term content is to indicate ideas—written or spoken, an object, a person, and the like.

The function of such objectives is to give guidance to teachers in the selection of learning activities and in the selection of evaluation techniques.

To summarize, an educational objective is a statement of purpose which describes possible and desirable student behavior which serve to give guidance to teachers in the selection of learning activities and evaluation techniques.

Learning Activities. Learning activities are those situations which are created by teachers and learners which allow learners to exhibit the behaviors described in an objective or objectives. There are many sources of criteria for judging activities. One set is by Goodlad in the 1959 ASCD Yearbook, *Learning and the Teacher* (*1*). In passing, it should be noted that any activity can and should be designed so that individual learners may be given the opportunity to work toward different objectives.

Evaluation. Evaluation in this context is defined as the description of student progress toward educational objectives. The description is to be used in making and reviewing decisions about individual students and their program. Technically, the word derives from Latin to mean to extract the value from. Since objectives describe desirable student behavior, or valued student behavior, the relation between objectives and evaluation can be seen. Further, as learning activities are to be designed to offer learners opportunities to engage in the behavior described in the objective, the cycle from objectives to activities to evaluation back to objectives, and the mutual dependency of all three can be seen.

Evaluation Contrasted to Other Activities

Perhaps because educators have not been careful in using terms—for example, there is a doctoral dissertation on the definitions of curriculum—the term evaluation is understood on occasion to mean testing, measurement, and grading. This section attempts to clarify the differences among these terms.

Testing and Measurement. The major distinction to be made between evaluation and testing and/or measurement is a relation to educational objectives. While tests or other measures, for example, height and weight, may in fact relate specifically to objectives adopted by a teacher or a school system, this is not necessarily the case. In many instances standardized tests are developed by experts removed from any specific situation; therefore, tests may well be unrelated to the objectives adopted by any school or school system, and yet these tests are used as criteria for judging student performance. Such data may or may not be a reflection of the objectives sought.

Another major distinction between tests and evaluation as concepts is that, typically, tests are standardized on groups of children, described by the test makers, and reveal something about the progress of groups or individual students in relation to the "norming" populations. Evaluation, on the other hand, is the description of the progress of one individual toward certain objectives about which standardized information may not be available.

One more distinction is offered to clarify further the intent of the term evaluation. Quite often a test is designed to give evidence about a specific area or skill, for example, arithmetic computation or word recognition. Evaluation, on the other hand, is related to the whole array of objectives about which the school or teacher is concerned.

None of the foregoing should be taken to mean that tests and evaluation are not in any sense related. For indeed they are. Later this is dealt with in some detail.

Grading. In some cases one hears the terms *grading* and *evaluating* used synonymously. Let me quickly try to make the distinction between them. Evaluation results tell us how much progress has been made. A grade given for this progress tells the student whether the progress was enough, enough for an A or a B or even an F. The chief function of evaluation is to describe progress. Grading is an act of judging the quality or quantity of progress. Grading is sometimes done on the performance of one individual in terms of the progress of the group as a whole or in terms of the individual's progress in relation to his own ability. Evaluation yields evidence about an individual in relation to one or more objectives.

Characteristics of Evaluation

The following constitutes a description of the specific characteristics of evaluation, with illustrations of techniques where these are appropriate.

1. Evaluation, because it describes progress, assumes that knowledge is available regarding where each student began. That is, a single test at the end of a unit will not reveal much about progress unless the starting point of the individual is also known. Pre- and post-testing are sometimes done with a paper and pencil test in such an area as spelling. Initial testing is often defined as diagnosis, although the term *diagnosis* seems more negative than does the term *description* of a student's activity at the start of instruction. In "old-time" terms, this is how we find out where the student is so that we can take him as far as he can go. Without such initial information we cannot have evaluation.

2. Evaluation is a continuous process. If our interest is progress and not some sort of terminal behavior, or the acquisition of certain behaviors within a specified period of time, then we must collect evidence on student progress continuously. Only then are we sufficiently aware of the nature and direction of progress to be in a position to alter instructional strategies and environment so that progress for any individual student may be optimum for him.

3. Evaluation requires adequate samples of a student's work. For example, if we are concerned with a student's acquisition of particular physical skills, then we must have more than pre- and post-teaching data. For obvious reasons, what a student does today, because of a cold or virus, may not be representative of what he is actually able to do. Therefore, many samples of his efforts must be collected.

4. An evaluation technique must offer some promise that the student will be able to engage in the behavior called for by the objective toward which the learner is to be making progress. Tyler uses somewhat stronger language in saying that the evaluation situation must evoke or cause the student to emit the behavior under consideration (5). However, because certainty in such situations is a rarity, it seems sufficient that such a situation, at least upon close examination and logical analysis, could allow the student to engage in a given behavior.

    This is not meant to interpret the term *behavior* in any narrow, restricted, or terminal sense. Nor is it intended to imply that behavior must be acquired in a specified time. Nor is it to ascertain what constitutes the behaviors anyone must accept as desirable. This is a question to be left to individuals who are responsible for curriculum planning and the actual instruction of particular students.

Within this framework, behaviors may include inquiring, valuing, enjoying, communicating, loving, appreciating, as well as memorizing and comprehending. Parenthetically, recent studies tend to confirm earlier work which indicates that approximately 90 percent of teachers' classroom questions require students to engage in memorization and regurgitation of isolated information. Only 8 percent of the time, then, is available for having students engage in other behaviors, some of which were listed above.

If we are concerned in some fashion with learners' behavior (whatever behaviors are agreed upon by those whose responsibility it is to make such determinations), then the classroom environment must provide opportunities for the learner to engage in the behavior about which we claim to be concerned. Classroom environment includes materials, equipment, lighting, as well as the nature and quality of discourse between students and teacher and among students. While we can and consciously do control the more obvious aspects of this environment, research suggests that we do not, as teachers, consciously control the dialogue in relation to the behaviors we say learners should acquire. What we say, both in classroom discussion and on examinations, tends to ignore many of the behaviors in which we claim to be interested.

This point seems too obvious to belabor; yet it is likely violated more frequently than any other requirement of evaluation. That is, regardless of what we claim to be interested in having youngsters accomplish—whether it be critical thinking, analysis, synthesis, or appreciation—the evaluation situations into which we put them require them to spout back to us, usually in the same form, bits and pieces of information. Furthermore, in far too many cases we insist that the information be acquired by a certain time in the child's school career or, if not, that he be required to repeat a grade. It is difficult to square this practice with the notions of progress and continuity mentioned earlier.

5. Evaluation is, in itself, a learning situation. An evaluation situation must allow a student to see himself in a new light, to learn something new about what progress he has made and in what new directions he might move. This implies that he in some fashion shares in the evaluation and the results thereof.
6. Finally, evaluation is open-ended. That is, an evaluation situation or technique opens new doors and points ahead rather than backward. It does not allow a learner to feel, "Now that's finished." These final two points are directly related to the whole concept of continuous evaluation.

To summarize the characteristics of evaluation, it describes beginnings as well as progress; it is continuous; it utilizes many samples of a learner's work; it allows the student to engage in the particular behavior or behaviors toward which he is assumed to be moving; it constitutes a learning situation; and it is open-ended, indicating new directions.

Some Illustrative Evaluation Techniques

It is impossible to enumerate all evaluation techniques here. Among the wide variety available are tests, situations, anecdotal records, measurement, and other paper and pencil items.

Tests. In almost any area one can find tests designed to measure achievement of students. One only need take a superficial look through any edition of the *Mental Measurements Yearbook* to see what is available. In many cases, more than one form of the same instrument is published. Where this is true, it is somewhat simpler to determine where an individual is at the outset of instruction and where he is at the conclusion. One must be certain that the test measures those factors which are considered to be important by the school system and which are, in the estimation of those responsible for evaluation, related to those behaviors toward which the schools are working. In some instances, an examination of a test, or tests, may disclose that the school is, in fact, overlooking some areas to which it thought it was giving attention.

If it is possible to locate a test which is a true "fit" in a given situation, and if individual students do not do well after instruction, evaluation, and judgment, it could be the case that what is sought is not clear to teachers or that instruction has been inadequate or that a given student has a problem heretofore unrecognized.

The foregoing has related to commercial tests. Much the same could be said for teacher-made tests of a paper and pencil variety.

If one accepts the description of behaviors in the Cognitive Taxonomy, then it is possible to develop paper and pencil items for all six behaviors listed. This is not as true for affective behaviors. One might hypothesize that we've had a great deal more practice in testing mental behaviors than we have had in testing appreciations, values, and the like; thus we are infinitely more proficient at describing and/or agreeing upon definitions of the more "mental" behaviors. It should be recalled that the cognitive behaviors are knowledge of specifics, comprehension, application, analysis, synthesis, and evaluation.

Since we claim to be concerned with something more than cognitive learning; that is, we speak often of values, appreciations, interests, attitudes, skills, and the like, then one might raise a question as to the appropriateness of paper and pencil tests in relation to these behaviors.

Situations. Let us consider for a moment the question of appreciation of "good" literature. What kind of evaluation situation or technique makes sense in this context? What kind of question on a paper test would measure a student's appreciation? This is not to say that such is impossible. I would, however, raise a question as to whether we know anymore than what a student is willing to write. And certainly we have all heard about the test-wise student. If we can believe what students state at the college level, they have learned to play the game and quite honestly inquire as to what is wanted. Once they have found out what is wanted, they will then do it. Or if we can believe some research, we might be concerned to learn that somewhere during third grade children show evidence of ceasing to be question askers and become question answerers. All this is to intimate that in some instances, paper and pencil tests are not reliable indicators of student attitudes, values, etc.

What constitutes a reasonable alternative when we are concerned with such attributes as interest? One is to arrange situations in which a student can choose from among a variety of activities. For example, a teacher may set up a music listening center, a "free reading" table, a science table, and a film strip center. If a student consistently chooses one, the teacher might conclude that the student is interested in that activity.

The problem here is reaching some agreement as to what sorts of behaviors we are willing to say make up an attitude, a value, or an interest. Since evaluation is largely a description of an individual, a teacher might include in the student's record that he is interested in music and then give reasons why the teacher thinks so. Others may not agree with what the teacher reports as evidence of interest on the part of the student, but at least persons reading the report will have some basis for agreeing or disagreeing and will have some description of the way in which a given student acts in relation to music.

Anecdotal records. These records constitute another evaluation technique. Such records must meet the conditions of evaluation spelled out earlier, including initial information, continuity, open-endedness, and the others.

One factor related to anecdotal records is critical-objectivity. Frequently, the social behavior of youngsters is of importance in a school situation, important enough to be graded on a report to parents. The grade may be a check or a minus; it may be a U for unsatisfactory or an S for satisfactory; or it may be a 1, 2, or 3. Whatever the grading system, the specific grade should be based upon evidence which is relevant to the behavior under consideration. Such evidence should be as free as possible from judgment. That is, the record should be as objective as it is humanly possible to make it. The time for judgment is when the grade is awarded, not when evidence is being collected. In such records, one should not find such words as *good* or *bad* or *trouble maker* or *a joy to have in class*. As with the question of interest, the particular behaviors which lead one teacher to the conclusion that a child is *bad* may well lead another teacher to the conclusion that the child is *exciting*. Thus, records should include description, not judgment. They should also be kept on a continuing basis, and should include many samples of what a given student does so that his behavior in many situations is recorded. I have yet to see a child who is never acceptable to me. If, however, his behavior is usually disturbing to me, I am liable to overlook the times when he is not disturbing. He is entitled to have me sample all his variety of behaviors.

Measurement. Related to testing, in a sense, is measurement. As the term is used here, it entails records of a different sort. Whether one keeps such records depends to a large extent upon what is seen as desirable in a given situation. In any case, such records as height, weight, vision, hearing, and the like are appropriate. Assuming that growth is important, without determining the precise amount to be exhibited, then records showing such progress can be useful in the overall picture of an individual.

Other Paper and Pencil Instruments. There are other paper and pencil instruments which are different from the tests mentioned above. These include interest inventories, actual written work of individuals, art work, and lists of books read. These may be useful as evidence when identifying interests or attitudes.

Where at all possible other sources of evidence (and that is all any technique is) should be employed. These new sources include films, audio tapes, and video tapes. The appropriateness of these in relation to speaking, reading, and self-expression in dramatics is clear.

Certainly there are other techniques available. The ones mentioned here are intended to indicate the breadth of possibilities and to underscore the need for a wide variety of techniques of evaluation.

Responsibilities in an Evaluation Program

The first step in building a program of evaluation is to determine to what extent evaluation is desired. In this context evaluation is not testing alone, nor is it grading, nor is it reporting. While all these may be related, they are not identical unless they happen to be defined as such in a local situation. The questions related to grading and reporting, along with promoting and retaining, require answers to a different set of questions. Therefore, for example, to plan a rather broad program of standardized testing is not to plan a comprehensive program of evaluation unless the standardized tests measure those factors and all those factors described in the objectives. Further, it should be remembered here that evaluation relates more directly to individual progress than to group progress. Another element in taking the first step is to stipulate what use will be made of evaluation results. Examples of such use include appraisal of teacher effectiveness, appraisal of objectives (are they realistic for this system), appraisal of materials, appraisal of class size or grouping practices, reporting to parents, and perhaps most important, working with each individual so that his educational environment is tailored to his needs. These decisions will determine what kind of records and how many need to be kept and by whom; where records are to be sent or kept; and who needs what information and in what form.

Here it is important to recognize and maintain a distinction between evaluation itself and the use to be made of the evidence collected during evaluation. While the distinction seems obvious, it is nonetheless the case that often the two terms are telescoped and the individual student is lost in the total program.

The following serves to illustrate. If evaluation data are to be used in appraising a total program within a school system only, then such data should be sent to a central office evaluator who might then appraise the total system and make such recommendations as "too much anxiety," "too little attention given to the arts," or to "independent reading," or to "physical education," or to some other objective which the system has established as desirable. If, on the other hand, teachers alone are to use evaluation data, such information can be kept by the individual teacher for use with individuals within his class. Obviously, these are not necessarily exclusive; evaluation data may be used in all the ways mentioned in any one situation. The point is, the use must be determined in each situation. With clarification comes an understanding of where responsibility lies for collection and use and a specification of areas where mutual use of data is to be made in the interest of each individual student. If a child's progress is minimal in one area but extensive in another, his achievement is not averaged. By analyzing a wide variety of evaluation data on an individual, there is less probability that undue pressure will be put on a student to make progress in one area when progress in another area might be more important for him. However, unless a wide spectrum of data is collected, there is little assurance that such pressure will not be unconsciously exerted. Although school systems assert an interest in the all-around development of individuals, information about individuals is typically limited to academic achievement, social behavior, and work habits. Exceptions to this overgeneralization are those students who exhibit behavior or learning problems.

Because of the nature of evaluation, and its close relation to objectives and classroom activities, it is impossible to talk about who should evaluate, and how, without treating to some extent the question of objectives.

Objectives include two elements: student behavior and content. These two terms are broadly conceived. The major function is to guide teachers in the selection of activities and evaluation techniques. If this function is to be served, it seems logical to involve teachers in the formulation of objectives. Teachers do sit on committees which are charged with stating objectives. As objectives are formulated, however, few are circulated among teachers to discover what teachers would do in the classroom in relation to the objectives. If the objectives are to communicate something to teachers then it seems reasonable to discover whether this something is in fact communicated. It matters not what the objectives are, but if they are to be emphasized in classrooms, then teachers should be able to understand the intent of an objective. The only way to find this out is to ask.

Two questions might well be asked of teachers: 1) Given a typical classroom, what *kinds* of activities would you offer to children to achieve this objective? The notion of kinds of activities in the plural is crucial; in most instances there is no one activity which will assure that an objective will be achieved nor any one activity that is appropriate for each individual as he works toward the objective. 2) What would you use as evidence to determine whether a student is making progress toward this objective? Or, how would you collect evidence to determine what progress a student is making?

Thus, the second step in building an evaluation program is to be clear about what objectives are important and whether teachers can use them as they are intended to be used. The responsibility for this step lies with the person responsible for curriculum development *and* teachers. It is not an either/or proposition.

The third major step in building an evaluation program is to exercise the imagination in relation to the types of techniques which are appropriate to a given objective. Certainly there are times when group tests are useful and relevant. There are, however, times when they cannot reveal what is needed. Critical to remember is that *whatever* techniques are employed, they allow only more or less sophisticated inferences to be made about an individual; conclusions, therefore, should be held tentatively. In any case, a real brainstorming session could be profitably held to suggest as many ways to evaluate, let us say, progress in art appreciation as a group can construct. Criteria for relevance of a technique will come out as the intent of the term appreciation becomes more clear as a result of the brainstorming. The responsibility for this step lies in the hands of the central office personnel who are in some way attached to program development and in the hands of teachers to whom the intent of objectives must be clear if relevant evidence is to be collected. When a satisfactory set of illustrative techniques has been established for any one or any set of objectives, they should be circulated along with the objectives to all teachers who will be expected to use them. Refinements can be made on the basis of responses. When a compilation has been made, a statement can then be accepted on a tentative basis. The basis is tentative because evaluation is continuous and, as evidence is collected, changes in objectives and techniques will be indicated.

The fourth step in building an evaluation program is to determine what kinds of data must be collected, how often it is to be collected, and with whom it is to be shared. For example, there may be certain academic skills which are acquired over a relatively short period of time. Thus, initial measures will be taken and reported, with one or more follow-up measures taken in a matter of weeks. If information about the permanence of learning or the extension of a skill is desired, additional measures, taken over a longer period of time, would be called for.

When interest is in something akin to appreciation of a certain type of literature or to the internalization of a particular value, if we can believe the evidence available to us, we need not expect rapid progress. Frequent collection of data regarding this kind of progress is not necessary. For assistance in making decisions regarding the timing of collection, a school staff might well employ the services of a psychologist. Whether data are shared only between teacher and child or are shared among teacher, child, and administrative personnel depends upon whether a particular kind of data are to be used for total program appraisal or for helping a given individual. This is a matter for local determination, but it is a question which must be raised.

The fifth step, and perhaps at once the most and least important, is to determine the form in which data should be collected and shared. One might even want to be so extreme as to standardize a form for anecdotal records or a vocabulary for describing progress in certain areas. This appears to be too confining, but some way of assuring accurate communication should be devised. The most efficient way to accomplish this is to ask those persons who are to use a document, test, or profile what it conveys to them. Since personnel changes fairly rapidly, this should be done regularly.

Finally, the last step in building an evaluation program is to *use* the data collected. No matter how specific the uses are, no matter how well documents communicate, and no matter how appropriate the particular technique, it all goes for naught unless it is used to help individuals make the progress of which they are capable.

Now to return to the beginning assertion. Hastings reports that in a study of 2,000 teachers in 591 schools, approximately 50 percent of these teachers look at test data or other information about their students. Payne's study (4) reveals that students who are unlikely to achieve acceptable levels of attainment under a given curricular arrangement can be identified and helped early in their school careers.

This study has supported the findings of other investigators who suggest that determinism does exist in schools. The relative positions of students within a group were established early and maintained over several years. Some change is necessary if the school is striving to bring all students to at least a minimal level of "satisfactory" achievement. The study has presented strong evidence that a change will not occur under the present practices in these schools . . . then a responsibility exists for identifying those students who are not likely to reach this level under existing conditions.

Thus, the rallying cry with regard to evaluation is, at the very least, to use what we already have in the way of data. Individual students, however, are entitled to better than the least we can do. Given our present sophistication, the best we can do is to collect relevant data so that conditions for individuals do not force them into slots, particularly when the slot is marked *failure*.

REFERENCES

1. Bloom, Benjamin S. *et al. Taxonomy of Educational Objectives-Handbook I: The Cognitive Domain.* New York: David McKay, 1956.
2. Goodlad, John I. "The Teacher Selects, Plans, and Organizes," *Learning and the Teacher*, 1959 Yearbook, Association for Supervision and Curriculum Development. Washington, D.C.: The Association, 1959, 39-60.
3. Krathwohl, David, *et al. Taxonomy of Educational Objectives-Handbook II: The Affective Domain.* New York: David McKay, 1964.
4. Payne, M. Arlene. "The Use Of Data in Curricular Decisions," unpublished doctoral dissertation, University of Chicago, 1963.
5. Tyler, Ralph W. *Basic Principles of Curriculum and Instruction.* Chicago: University of Chicago Press, 1950.

Thomas C. Barrett

UNIVERSITY OF WISCONSIN

2. Goals of the Reading Program: The Basis for Evaluation

SINCE the purpose of this Perspectives in Reading volume is to consider various dimensions and means of evaluating the reading behaviors of students, it seems appropriate to focus attention on the goals of the reading program which should provide the basis for the evaluative process. A prerequisite to this undertaking, however, is a common understanding of the definition of reading that will be used as a point of departure in the discussion of the goals of a reading program. Thus, this presentation will have two purposes. First, it will present contrasting definitions of reading and will delineate the definition which will constitute the foundation for the remainder of the chapter. Second, the discussion will deal with some selected goals of a reading program which appear to be important with respect to the definition.

What is Reading?

The necessity for dealing with the question, "What is Reading?" is based on two hypotheses: (a) that the term *reading* means different things to different people; and (b) that the way in which a teacher consciously or unconsciously defines reading is reflected in the goals of the reading program he provides for his youngsters. Whether these hypotheses can or cannot be validated empirically is open to question, but it does seem logical that the data for such an undertaking are available. For example, at the beginning of the semester I have each of the students enrolled in a graduate course in developmental reading write a definition of reading. As might be expected, the results are quite divergent. Moreover, the fact that different definitions of reading do exist in the minds of teachers suggests that it might be possible to observe the impact of these stated definitions in the goals they emphasize in their reading programs.

Although the argument as to whether the hypotheses can be validated empirically is purely academic at the moment, it is not speculation to state that the professional literature is replete with definitions of reading, that the definitions do in fact differ, and that they do have differing implications for instruction. In an extreme and somewhat facetious sense, an anecdote offered by Huey (5) in his early book, *The Psychology and Pedagogy of Reading* may help to illustrate the point:

> To the early peoples, reading was one of the most mysterious of the arts, both in its performance and in its origin. We recall how, even in modern times, Livingstone excited the wonder and awe of an African tribe as he daily perused a book that had survived the vicissitudes of travel. So incomprehensible, to these savages, was his performance with the book, that they finally stole it and ate it, as the best way they knew of "reading" it.

Whether Huey's anecdote can be accepted as a legitimate definition of reading is doubtful. Nevertheless, it would certainly simplify the task of determining the goals for a reading program.

In a more serious light, the literature related to the psychology and the teaching of reading reveals three points of view when it comes to defining reading: (a) reading is decoding; (b) reading involves perception and cognition; and (c) reading involves a perceptual response, a cognitive response and an affective response.

Reading is decoding. Bloomfield (2) among others presented the idea that reading is basically relating sounds to symbols. He contended that the alphabetic nature of the English language more or less demands that reading be viewed in this light. Furthermore, he suggested that meaning is not uniquely inherent to reading, but that it is related to all uses of language. The implication here is that to perceive reading as anything other than breaking a written code is to confuse the issue.

In its purest form, then, a decoding definition of reading indicates that the student must develop habit patterns which permit him to automatically transform written signals into their oral counterparts. In other words, the primary task of a teacher of reading, when this is the accepted definition of reading, is to enable pupils to develop an understanding of the alphabetic nature of the language and to develop, either inductively or deductively, skill in producing sounds for symbols. Thus, the implications the decoding definition of reading holds for the reading program are quite definite with respect to the operation of the teacher and his students. First, it seems reasonable that there would be a great deal of emphasis on sound-symbol relationships in such a classroom. Second, there undoubtedly would be a considerable amount of oral reading for the purpose of determining the accuracy of decoding. Finally, the reading program would deal with cognition only in an incidental way. These operations, it appears, would be standardized from group to group and from grade level to grade level.

Reading involves perception and cognition. In contrast to the decoding definition of reading are those definitions which view reading as a two dimensional act. Smith and Dechant (*10*) and DeBoer and Dallmann (*3*) as well as others have taken this position. The definitions which fall into this category suggest that reading involves not only visual perception of the written symbols, but also thoughtful responses on the part of the reader. They also imply that the intent of the reader and the background he has to work with in responding to what he reads will permit him to develop new understandings and modify old concepts.

The implications the two-dimensional definition holds for the reading program are far different from those projected by the decoding definition. Basically, it extends the concept of reading purveyed by the decoding definition by placing strong emphasis on meaning and levels of thought. Therefore, this definition suggests that the classroom teacher should be concerned with word perception skills and with the ability on the part of the reader to interact with the author in a variety of thoughtful ways. A reading program which is congruent with the two-dimensional definition would provide learning activities of this nature at all grade levels.

Reading involves perceptual, cognitive and affective responses. The third type of definition that can be found in the literature is more complex than either of the other two types. It suggests that reading has three dimensions; namely, a perceptual dimension, a meaning dimension, and an emotional dimension. With these criteria in mind, reading can be defined in the following manner:

> Reading involves the visual perception of written symbols and the transformation of the symbols to their explicit or implicit oral counterparts. The oral responses then act as stimuli for a thoughtful reaction on the part of the reader. The type or level of thought induced by the stimuli is determined, in part, by the intent and the background of the reader and the nature of the materials. In addition, the effort expended in the perceptual act and the intellectual impact of the written materials on the reader is influenced by his interest in the specific selection and by his attitude toward reading in general.

The definition of reading noted above has rather definite implications for a reading program. Basically, it suggests that a reading program which is congruent with this definition should have three strands. One strand should be concerned with the perceptual skills of reading. A second strand of the program should deal with the cognitive dimensions of reading, while a third strand should be devoted to the affective dimensions of reading. Not only should there be three strands in terms of goals for the reading program, but there should also be evidence of learning activities in the program which are explicitly designed to aid youngsters in attaining these goals. Thus, an analysis of the biweekly or monthly program, in terms of the time allotted to different endeavors, should reveal a relative balance with respect to the three strands of goals. An optimum balance would, of course, depend on the grade level and the types of pupils involved; nevertheless, the three strands should always be visible. Moreover, the ongoing evaluation of the reading program should focus attention on each of the three dimensions of the program. To clarify this position, the following sections present a more analytical discussion of the specific goals of the reading program using the three-dimensional definition as a conceptual framework.

Goals of the Reading Program

Educational goals have often been viewed as uninspiring fare by people who should be deeply concerned with them. This feeling may come from several sources. First, there are some people who consider goals to be the artifacts of some theoretician's thoughts. This reaction may come about because the goals are imposed on teachers from outside sources, such as curriculum guides and teachers' manuals. The end result is that teachers do not become ego involved with implementing goals, because they have had nothing to do with creating them.

A second possibility for the general lack of enthusiasm for goals is that they are frequently stated in such a fashion that they do not give adequate guidance to the person who is to help children accomplish them. In some cases, the goals are so gross that they leave a great deal of latitude for interpretation or misinterpretation. In other instances, they focus attention on teacher behavior and not on pupil behavior; thus, they distract the teacher's attention from behavioral outcomes on the part of his students and draw it to his teaching techniques. There is no doubt that a relationship exists between teaching technique and pupil behavior, but goals should be stated in terms of pupil behaviors so that attention is focused on the pupils primarily and on the teacher secondarily.

A third reason why educational goals appear to carry negative connotations may be that the relationships among the philosophy guiding the educational program, the goals of the program, instructional decisions governing the learning activities, and the evaluation process have not been clearly perceived. As a case in point, consider these relationships with respect to the reading program again. In this instance, the definition of reading provides the basis for the scope of the goals. The goals, in turn, indicate the kinds of reading and reading related behaviors that children should demonstrate as a result of the reading program. In other words, the goals of the program should guide the teacher in the types of learning activities he selects and the evaluation procedures he follows.

Although the remainder of the article will not resolve the problems inherent in a discussion of educational goals, what follows is designed to accomplish two things: (a) the goals of the reading program will be put into perspective with regard to the three-dimensional definition of reading; and (b) the nature and instructional implications of selected goals of the reading program will receive consideration.

Goals of the Reading Program in Perspective

In an effort to put the goals of the reading program into a frame of reference, Figure 1 was created. Specifically, it was designed (a) to show the relationships of the goals to the operational definition, the implementation of the goals, and the evaluation process and (b) to provide some descriptive information about the categories of goals and their relationship to one another.

Figure 1 shows that, in the first instance, the flow of action, as indicated by the arrows, is from the definition of reading, to the goals, to the implementation of the goals, to the evaluation of the desired reading behaviors, and back to the goals. This suggests that within certain limits the program has some flexibility in as much as the results of the evaluation may give new directions to some goals and may suggest increased emphasis on others. Such changes in these elements will have a direct influence on the types of and time allotted to certain learning activities. This circular flow of action is constant and is what keeps the reading program up-to-date.

With regard to the second purpose of Figure 1, it should be noted that the three categories of goals are briefly described so that they reflect the essence of the instructional goals appropriate to each dimension of the program. For example, the perceptual dimension of the program is concerned with skills in word perception. Although perception is used rather broadly here, the intent of this dimension of the program is rather precise, since it focuses on the ability of children to demonstrate flexibility, accuracy, and variability of rate in word perception. The cognitive dimension of the program, on the other hand, indicates that children should demonstrate different levels of thought in their reading. Finally, the affective goals of the reading program deal with the child's feelings about reading, particularly the feelings that reading is worthwhile and self-fulfilling.

In addition, Figure 1 shows that the three types of goals are interrelated. The implication here is that the type or level of thought demonstrated by the reader is dependent on his perceptual skills and on his feelings about reading at the moment or in general. Moreover, how well a child under-

FIGURE I

INTERACTIONS AMONG A DEFINITION OF READING,
CATEGORIES OF GOALS OF THE READING PROGRAM,
IMPLEMENTATION OF THE GOALS,
AND EVALUATION OF PUPILS' READING AND
READING RELATED BEHAVIORS

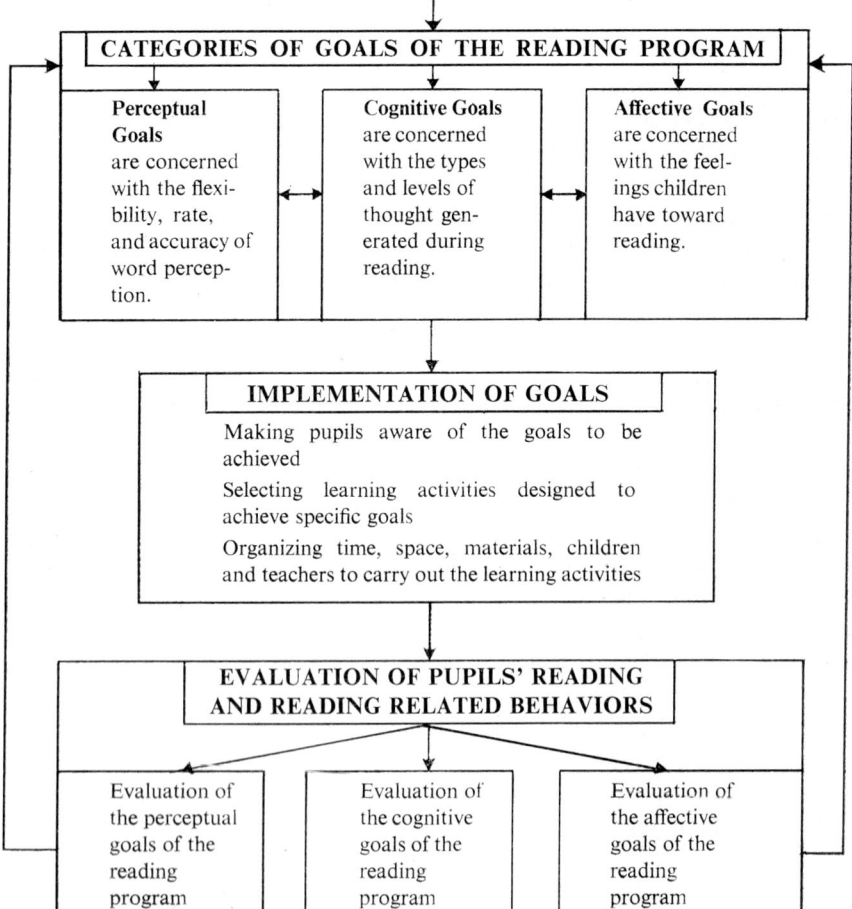

stands what he is reading and the way he feels about reading influences his efforts in the perceptual area. In other words, the three types of goals and their behavioral outcomes do interact and are interdependent upon one another. This does not preclude the possibility, however, that we can think about and organize the reading program in such a way that the three types of goals will receive varying degrees of emphasis at different times.

In general, then, the purpose of Figure 1 is to support the position that the goals of the reading program should be three-dimensional in nature and that the goals are interdependent on one another and interrelated with a definition of reading, the implementation of the goals, and the evaluation process.

In order to further clarify the significance of the goals of the reading program, the remainder of the presentation will be devoted to a discussion of some selected goals, their implementation, and their implications for evaluation.

Perceptual Goals of the Reading Program

Although this dimension of the reading program sometimes becomes cluttered with the listing of a variety of skills, it seems appropriate for the purpose of the present undertaking to focus on word perception only. What, then, do we want pupils to accomplish with respect to word perception? Without going into great detail, it seems that the reading program should have three basic objectives in this area. Stated in behavioral terms, they are (a) pupils should be able to use a variety of techniques to perceive words; (b) pupils should demonstrate accuracy in perceiving words; and (c) pupils should demonstrate the ability to adjust the rate of word perception to the reading task. Although all three of the goals are important, only the first goal will be discussed at this point, since it is the most fundamental of the three listed.

That children should possess a variety of ways to perceive and identify words is a goal of long standing. However, over a period of time, there have been arguments that too much emphasis has been given to one type of word perception skill while too little emphasis has been given to another type. Such arguments cannot and should not be generalized across the board, since the perceptual skills that should be emphasized with one child or one group of children may not be appropriate for all children. This is where the teacher's professional judgment must come into play. The teacher must emphasize certain perceptual skills on the basis of his knowledge of his pupils' needs, his knowledge of the various techniques that can be used to perceive words, and his knowledge of the types of behaviors he wants youngsters to demonstrate in this area. In other words, the skills emphasized must result from a thoughtful analysis of the perceptual techniques needed by children. This position is as true for first grade as it is for sixth grade.

One of the problems faced with respect to the goal that children should be able to demonstrate a variety of ways to perceive words is that some teachers do not have the knowledge needed to be analytical. In my experience with teachers who have enrolled in a graduate course in reading, it is not uncommon to find at the beginning of the course, as many as 40 percent of the members of a class who cannot define such terms as context clues, sight words, structural analysis, blend, digraph, and syllable. Nor is it unusual to find that there is little or no knowledge of at least one common sequence of teaching phonic skills; that is, in one common sequence the order of learnings is, initial consonants, final consonants, digraphs and blends, vowels, and syllables.

In another but related vein, it is not uncommon to find that experienced teachers of reading have little or no feeling for or understanding of possible pre-learnings that will facilitate a child's learning of a new technique for perceiving words. For example, the question, "What are two or three prerequisite skills for learning to syllabicate words?" draws a blank. Appropriate responses, such as, the ability to recognize the vowels and consonants in the alphabet, the ability to perceive vowel sounds in words, and the ability to apply certain vowel generalizations to single syllable words, go unmentioned.

Even in the case of first grade teachers, the concepts of helpful pre-learnings before actual reading instruction begins are vague. Although visual and auditory discrimination may be verbalized by some as being of value as prerequisite learnings, when the point is pressed as to how such skills might be developed and evaluated, the responses show no real grasp or understanding of the skills mentioned.

The purpose, here, is not to ridicule, although this may appear to be the case, rather it is to suggest that, if a legitimate goal of the perceptual dimension of the reading program is to have children learn to use a variety of techniques to perceive words, teachers must become more knowledgeable and more analytical with regard to these techniques. Once this is done, teachers will have greater facility in developing specific goals in this area which in turn will give more precise direction to instructional decisions and evaluation procedures.

Cognitive Goals of the Reading Program

The second dimension of the reading program deals with cognition or comprehension. The overriding goal here, it seems, is to enable pupils to grow in their ability to think about and react to written materials in a variety of ways. This goal has not always been achieved, for at least three reasons.

First, reading comprehension has been thought of as a general ability. This concept has been prompted, in part, by studies which have indicated the problems of measuring different types of reading comprehension. It also has been supported by the definition that reading is "getting meaning from the printed page." To get meaning, in this case, has been interpreted to mean ability to recall or recognize literal meanings only.

A second reason why readers have not become as thoughtful and as sensitive as some people would want them to be is that comprehension has been described as a fragmented ability with many minute sub-abilities. Such definitions of comprehension have produced so many elements that it is humanly impossible to keep them all in mind, let alone provide appropriate learning activities and evaluation techniques for all of them. The end result here has appeared in reading programs where there was little continuity in the cognitive dimension.

A third problem in this area seems to be that reading experts and authors of instructional materials have treated reading comprehension in different ways. Of particular concern, in this instance, is the lack of agreement in the terminology used. As a result, it is difficult to differentiate among such terms as creative reading, interpretive reading, and critical reading or to design tasks which will enable students to develop these abilities.

In an effort to overcome these problems, it might be well to consider a classification system which would provide an understandable and manageable basis for developing specific goals, selecting learning activities, and designing evaluative techniques for the cognitive strand of the reading program.

Using some of the categories and ideas developed by Bloom (1), Sanders (9), Letton (7), and Guszak (4), it seems appropriate to suggest that the goals for the cognitive dimension of the program could be placed into four categories: (a) literal meaning, (b) inference, (c) evaluation, and (d) appreciation. Let us briefly consider each of these categories.

Literal meaning. As used here, literal meaning is concerned with ideas and information which are explicitly stated in a reading selection. In terms of pupil behavior there are two types of literal meaning tasks. The first of these is recognition. Generally, a recognition task grows out of the purposes set for reading by either the teacher or the pupil. Such tasks require the student to locate or identify ideas or information explicitly stated in the reading selection itself or in exercises which use the explicit ideas and information presented in the reading selection. Recall is the second type of literal meaning task. In this instance the student is asked to produce from memory ideas and information explicitly stated in the reading selection.

Although literal meaning is the most basic level in the proposed classification system, purposes for reading and teachers' questions designed to elicit responses at this level may range from simple to complex. For example, a simple task in literal comprehension may be the recognition or recall of a single fact or incident in a story. On the other hand, a more complex task might be the recognition or recall of a series of facts or the sequencing of incidents in a reading selection.

Inference. The second category in the suggested classification system for reading comprehension deals with the ability to draw inferences. Inferential comprehension is demonstrated by the student when he uses the ideas and information explicitly stated in the selection, his intuition, and his personal experience as a basis for conjectures and hypotheses. Inferences drawn by the student may be either convergent or divergent in nature and the student may or may not be asked to verbalize the rationale underlying his inferences. In general, then, inferences are stimulated by purposes for reading and teachers' questions which demand thinking and imagination that go beyond the printed page.

There are a number of specific inferential tasks which readers might be asked to perform. For example, the student may be called upon to infer likenesses and differences in characters, times, or places as presented in the story with their counterparts in his memory. Such inferential comparisons can revolve around ideas such as here and there and now and then. Inferring cause and effect relationships is a second possibility. This endeavor may, for instance, require hypotheses about the reasons why characters interacted with time, places, and other characters in the way that they did. A third inferential task might be to deal with character traits. In this case the student is asked to hypothesize about the nature of characters on the basis of explicit clues presented in the selection. Character traits, as used here, may be psychological, sociological or physiological in nature. A final example of an inferential task would be predicting outcomes. This type of exercise is rather common and it occurs when students read an initial portion of a selection and conjecture about what will take place next.

In general, then, inference goes beyond what is explicitly stated in the materials read, and the quality of the inference is dependent on the literal meanings the reader obtains from the selection, on his reservoir of information, and on his flexibility of thinking.

Evaluation. Purposes for reading and teachers' questions, in this instance, require responses by the student which indicate that he has arrived at a judgment by comparing ideas presented in the selection with external criteria provided by the teacher, other authorities or other written sources, or with internal criteria provided by the reader's experiences, knowledge, or values. In essence, evaluation deals with judgments and focuses on qualities of correctness, worthwhileness, appropriateness, feasibility, and validity.

There are many opportunities to have students think about their reading at this level. Judgments concerning reality or fantasy are one basic type of task. When children are asked, "Do you think that pigs can really talk?" they are required to make a judgment on the basis of personal experience. Another example of an evaluation task is the one where a pupil might be asked to pass judgment on the adequacy and validity of a piece of writing on the basis of a comparison with other selections on the same subject. A third activity might be concerned with fact versus opinion, while a fourth task could deal with the appropriateness of a character's behavior. Other examples could be presented; however, the point is that the possibilities for evaluation do exist and should be utilized at all grade levels.

Appreciation. The fourth and final category in the suggested classification system involves all the previously mentioned levels of thought, and yet, it goes beyond them. Appreciation, as used here, calls for the student to be emotionally and aesthetically sensitive to the written work and to have a reaction to its psychological and artistic elements. For example, when a student verbalizes his feelings about part or all of a reading selection in terms of excitement, fear, dislike, or boredom, he is functioning at the appreciational level. This is also true when the reader demonstrates his sensitivity to, sympathy for, or empathy with characters and happenings portrayed by the author. Finally, appreciation occurs when the reader reacts to the author's artistic ability to paint word pictures which cause the reader to visualize, smell, taste, and hear. Although the behavioral products of specific appreciational goals may be difficult to evaluate, a concern for this type of intellectual and emotional response should be evident in the reading program.

In general, then, the suggested classification system for the cognitive dimension of the reading program provides direction for four types of specific goals in comprehension: *literal, inferential, evaluative,* and *appreciational.* Although there is overlap among these levels of thought, it appears that comprehension tasks can be designed which will place emphasis on responses that can be placed into the four categories. Moreover, it is hoped that, although literal comprehension is fundamental to the other types of comprehension, greater emphasis will be placed on inference, evaluation, and appreciation in future reading programs.

Affective Goals of the Reading Program

As the three-dimensional definition of reading indicated, the feelings a pupil has about a specific reading selection or about reading in general will have an influence on both the perceptual and cognitive dimensions of the reading act. Some people may be skeptical about the power of affective responses to influence reading. There will be others, however, who will nod their heads in approval, for they will have seen this phenomenon in operation. In a related vein, Theodore Clymer, at a recent University of Wisconsin Institute in Reading, discussed some readability research he had conducted. He found that a number of trade books that were recommended for primary grade use by the publishers went beyond the difficulty limits of a common readability formula designed for primary grade material. Yet, he noted, that children in the primary grades apparently read the books. The point of these remarks is to suggest that the affective responses of pupils to reading do have powerful influences on what is read and how it is read. It follows then, if one accepts this position, that affective goals should be included in the reading program.

As Krathwohl, Bloom, and Masia (6) have reported, affective goals generally deal with interests, attitudes, and values. They also have suggested that the behaviors related to these terms are very complex and that it is difficult to state goals for them, to implement the stated goals, and to evaluate the resulting behavior. Nevertheless, there appear to be at least two goals in this area that warrant some attention.

Reading interests. There is general agreement that pupils should broaden their reading interests as a result of the reading program. This goal suggests that an active effort should be made to make students aware of the variety of subjects and ideas about which people write. Awareness of the existence of the variety of avenues that a reader can follow is only the beginning. Even more important is the act of involving pupils in reading materials that they would not pursue if they were left to their own devices. It is hypothesized that, if pupils are exposed to and involved in the broad horizons of reading, they will respond to new reading tasks with more enthusiasm. In a sense, broadening reading interests is like broadening eating interests. If we try new foods often enough and find a few exciting new tastes in the process, we probably put more enthusiasm into trying other unknown foods.

There are a number of activities which may help to increase pupils' reading interests. Systematic oral reading by the teacher is one possibility. By systematic, it is meant that teachers should devote some time to this enterprise each day and that they should carefully select the materials they read so that their students are exposed to a broad variety of topics, types of materials, and styles of writing.

A second type of activity which can contribute to the broadening of interests is the procedure of having children share their reading with one another. Many specific ideas are available: (a) oral book reports; (b) oral reading of selected passages; (c) illustrated book reports; (d) auctioning books; and (e) a classroom "Saturday Review." There are other activities that could be suggested; however, the idea is that a child will be inclined to try something he might not have tried if a classmate had not made him aware of it.

Positive attitudes toward reading. The second goal of concern is that pupils will develop positive attitudes toward reading as a result of what is done in the reading program. Attitudes, in this instance, can range from just thinking kindly about reading to the point where reading will be selected as a leisure time activity when other alternatives are available. When one thinks about ways to achieve this goal, it is important to remember that it takes time to condition attitudes. Thus, whatever is done in a reading program to implement this goal must be done over an extended period of time.

With this in mind, one possible extended activity is to encourage children to pursue their reading interests through self-selection of materials and independent reading of the materials selected. Although self-selection of materials as an activity is rather common in many classrooms, it is rather uncommon to find relatively large blocks of time allotted to independent reading. Certainly, if we want children to feel that independent reading is worthwhile, we must demonstrate that we feel it is important by providing blocks of time in the weekly reading program for this purpose. It is not enough to say to students, "Select a book, take it home and read it."

Although this may be viewed as a plea for individualized reading in every classroom, it should not be. Rather it is a plea to permit children to have the opportunity to become acquainted with reading during school in a way that will prompt them to give it a high priority as an out-of-school activity. The name applied to such an endeavor is unimportant as long as it is done.

One final observation must be made with regard to interests and attitudes. It is that we must place more emphasis on the goals of the affective dimension of the program, for if we continue to ignore them or to exclude them we may find that we have thrown the baby out with the bath water.

Conclusion

The general purpose of this chapter was to provide a framework for thinking about goals of the reading program and to suggest, if only by implication, that the goals selected, whatever they may be, should provide the basis for evaluation. In attempting to achieve the objective, certain subjective judgments were made. Undoubtedly, some things were emphasized that should not have been, while other things were not mentioned that should have been. Hopefully, though, the discussion put some old and some new ideas about the goals of a reading program into better perspective.

REFERENCES

1. Bloom, Benjamin S., *et al. Taxonomy of Educational Objectives-Handbook I: Cognitive Domain.* New York: David McKay Company, Inc., 1956.
2. Bloomfield, Leonard, and Clarence L. Barnhart. *Let's Read.* Detroit: Wayne University Press, 1961.

3. DeBoer, John J., and Martha Dallmann. *The Teaching of Reading.* New York: Holt, Rinehart and Winston, Inc., 1961.
4. Guszak, Frank James. *Relations Between Teacher Practice and Knowledge of Reading Theory in Selected Grade School Classes* (USOE Cooperative Research Project No. S-437). Madison, Wisconsin: University of Wisconsin, 1966.
5. Huey, Edmund Burke. *The Psychology and Pedagogy of Reading.* New York: The Macmillan Company, 1908.
6. Krathwohl, David R., *et al. Taxonomy of Educational Objectives-Handbook II: Affective Domain.* New York: David McKay Company, Inc., 1964.
7. Letton, Mildred C. "Evaluating the Effectiveness of Teaching Reading," *Evaluation of Reading*, Helen M. Robinson, Editor, Supplementary Educational Monographs, No. 88. Chicago: The University of Chicago Press, December, 1958, pp. 76-82.
8. Otto, Wayne, Theodore L. Harris, and Thomas C. Barrett. *Transfer Effects of Training Intermediate Grade Pupils to Adjust Reading Speed to Reading Purpose* (USOE Cooperative Research Project No. 3137). Madison, Wisconsin: University of Wisconsin, 1966.
9. Sanders, Norris M. *Classroom Questions.* New York: Harper and Row, 1966.
10. Smith, Henry P., and Emerald V. Dechant. *Psychology in Teaching Reading.* Englewood Cliffs, N. J.: Prentice-Hall, Inc., 1961.

Dolores Durkin

UNIVERSITY OF ILLINOIS

3. Informal Techniques for the Assessment of Prereading Behavior

Papers are always difficult to write. The difficulty of this one was compounded by the immediate need to struggle with the meaning and therefore the focus of the assigned topic. In particular, I found myself struggling with the word *informal* and with the term *prereading*. What is an informal evaluative technique; and, in addition, what is prereading behavior? First, let me deal with the word *informal*, if only because I can give my own interpretation of what this means much more quickly than I can dispose of what might be meant by prereading.

Meaning of *Informal*

I am sure it would be accurate to say that the difficulties I experienced in coming to terms with the meaning of the word *informal* reflect my involvement, during the past few years, in the controversy about when to begin reading instruction. Because of my research with children who learned to read before entering school (4), I have been both invited and dragged into discussions about the advisability of introducing reading during the kindergarten year. In these discussions, I have observed, those who are opposed to reading for five-year-olds inevitably war against what they refer to as *formal* instruction. Although no specific definition is offered, it becomes clear that this formal instruction is *bad*. Evidently—by inference—informal instruction must be *good*, or at least *better*.

Because the terms *formal* and *informal* are so frequently used and so rarely defined—even in what I would say have been important discussions—I have often wondered whether I was the only one for whom they were not self-explanatory descriptions. And so, out of curiosity, but also to insure better communication, I recently asked a group of graduate students enrolled in one of my courses to distinguish between formal and informal instruction in reading. As it turned out, the request led to an interesting discussion in which it became quickly apparent that there were as many definitions of formal and informal instruction as there were students in the class. Out of this diversity, I must add, there came the resolution to avoid such labels, for they were clearly noncommunicative. Now, perhaps, with this little bit of background you can understand why I have had such difficulty preparing this paper.

Informal Evaluative Techniques

Having been given the task of dealing with informal evaluative techniques at the prereading level, let me start off with an attempt to arrive at some specific meaning for the term *informal*. Actually, in this particular instance a meaning can be derived simply by examining all of the topics considered in this volume on evaluation. These topics, as you have seen, divide not only into evaluations concerned with different dimensions and levels of reading; but they divide also into evaluations based on tests and evaluations described as informal. Thus, in this context it is appropriate to view informal techniques as a residual classification which includes any way of arriving at evaluative information other than by tests.

Before any misunderstanding develops, it should be emphasized that any reference to informal techniques as being whatever is "left over" after tests are excluded is not meant to be derogatory. As you will see much more clearly as this discussion moves along, any hope I have for the emergence of better evaluation at the beginning stages of reading is rooted not in tests but in informal techniques. I personally believe, as a matter of fact, that many of the tests we continue to use—and I think this is especially true of readiness tests—are leftovers from an earlier era that was characterized by a very naive faith in the validity and so-called "objectivity" of test scores.

For instance, if you have taken even an undergraduate course in testing and measurement, you are aware that back in the 1920's and the 1930's both educators and psychologists went through a period in which they showed what now seems like unbelievable naiveté about the value of test scores in assessing human characteristics and achievements. While the passing of time has fashioned some of this oversimplified thinking into a more sophisticated and realistic understanding of the complexities of human behavior, some residue from those earlier years remains. Reflecting it, I think, is the still too common belief that there is something uniquely clairvoyant and, in the case of readiness tests, even predictive about test scores. As a result of such beliefs we have children who are classified and labeled—for instance, *ready* or *unready, slow* or *bright, creative* or *non-creative*—simply because of their performance on tests which, if examined carefully, might prove to be neither objective nor valid.

Reasons for Using Tests

To make the charge that test scores continue to be used in our schools because of a limited understanding of the power of tests is to present an incomplete characterization of current practices in evaluation. Other common reasons for the continued use of test scores—for instance, to assess a child's readiness to read—relate to such facts as the following: tests are relatively simple to administer; they are efficient, when given to a group of children; the scores resulting from them are easily noted on a child's cumulative record card; and, in addition, the scores are "precise," "neat," and therefore "useful" in parent-teacher conferences. It is these attributes rather than the factor of validity which have led to the continued use of readiness tests over as many as thirty-five years—in spite of the fact that throughout this long period of time the value of readiness test scores as predictors of success with reading have been seriously questioned in one research report after another. (The author of the following chapter, Robert Dykstra, has recently written an excellent article for the *Reading Research Quarterly* (5) in which he not only reviews some of this literature but adds support to it with his own study of readiness assessment.)

Other Ways to Assess Readiness

Having raised these questions about the value of test scores for assessing a child's readiness to begin to read, I now face the obligation of proposing alternative ways for making decisions about when to start reading instruction. However, before moving to other possibilities I would first like to focus attention on still another term in the title of this presentation which caused me some mental anguish. It is the description *prereading*. What is *prereading behavior?*

Meaning of Prereading

I suppose it is the occasional need I feel to use my three years of high school Latin which suggests that a consideration of the meaning of prereading ought to begin with attention to the prefix *pre*. As you know, this prefix indicates something that comes before, either in place (*pre*fix) or in time (*pre*arrange). In the case of the word *prereading*, it would seem to indicate something that exists before a child starts to read. Implied in such a dictionary definition, of course, is the idea that prereading behavior and reading behavior occur at separate points on some time line. Apparent within this framework is the traditional interpretation of the concept of reading readiness which, from its inception in the 1920's, encouraged the belief that getting a child ready to read and teaching him to read occur at separate times in his school life (*1, 6*).

Because my own viewpoint is different and because it is directly related to what I will propose as the best evaluative technique at the beginning stages of reading, I want to take time now to discuss my particular interpretation of *readiness*, in this instance applied to learning to read.

Reading Readiness

Traditionally, persons attempting to define readiness have viewed it as a product; for instance, in the beginning it was assumed to be the product of maturation (*7, 9*). Viewing readiness as a product is defensible, but current knowledge indicates that a child's readiness to learn to read—or, more generally, his capacity for learning—is the product both of maturation and of environmental factors (*3, 8*). Within this framework, then, reading readiness can be defined as that capacity for learning to read which results from nature and nurture interacting on each other.

To view readiness as a product is helpful, but to view it only as a product is to suffer the error of incompleteness. What must be added to the definition of readiness seen as a product is that dimension which brings into focus the relationship between a child's capacity to learn to read and the kind of learning opportunities made available to him. Within this framework readiness is still a product, but it is a product in relation to a given set of circumstances. Or, to use the words of another writer, readiness is "the adequacy of existing capacity in relation to the demands of a given learning task" (*2*).

Assessment of Readiness

Outlining these two dimensions of readiness—readiness as a product and readiness as a relationship—brings into focus some obvious implications for school assessments of a child's readiness to read. Clearly apparent, for instance, is the oversimplification of assessments which use a single-factor criterion such as chronological age or, as was once commonly suggested, mental age. Equally apparent, though, is the inadequacy of any attempt to assess readiness apart from the kind of reading instruction that will be available.

But, let me turn the focus around and deal with the positive implications of this view of readiness. What is its meaning for elementary school administrators and teachers who must deal with the question, "When should reading begin?" If a chronological age of six is no longer defensible as *the* criterion for starting instruction and, secondly, if it is likely that particular combinations of maturation and environmental factors produce high learning capacities in some five-year-olds, then one positive implication is that the kindergarten year is the time to begin efforts in assessing readiness. In addition, if readiness can only be established in relation to "the demands of a given learning task," then another positive implication is that an assessment of readiness during the kindergarten year will be most reliable when it comes from the combination of (a) a situation offering varied opportunities to learn to read; and (b) a knowledge of what individual children are able to learn from the opportunities offered.

Examples of Assessment

To insure specific understanding of the kind of diagnostic situation that has just been proposed it might be helpful, at this point in the discussion, to include a few illustrations of "kindergarten opportunities to learn to read." One immediate difficulty in choosing illustrations is the lack of realism in thinking about kindergarten in terms of a single kind of program. To be sure, there is always the temptation to believe that kindergarten is still comprised of the experiences we ourselves had as five-year-olds; but visits to schools in the 1960's show anything but one kind of program. Some kindergartens, for instance, have swung over to an imitation of the first grade in their use of reading workbooks and basal readers. And, of course, it is just this kind of wholesale, unimaginative swing that has engendered opposition to reading during the kindergarten year—opposition, it must be added, which rarely distinguishes between a method that might be inappropriate but a timing that might be just right, at least for some kindergartners.

Regardless, though, of these variations in particular programs, it still is realistic to assume that certain things go on in every kindergarten. For instance, it is probably accurate to assume that some time in every kindergarten is given to the job of taking attendance. Mundane and routine though it is, attendance-taking can provide the opportunity for five-year-olds to recognize their names when "written down"—although here it must be emphasized that some of these children will already be far beyond just knowing their names. Nonetheless, beginning with the showing of names by a teacher and concluding later in the school year with each child indicating his presence by selecting his name card and putting it on an attendance board, this simple but necessary routine could teach a child to read his name and, probably, other names as well. But—and this is the point to be emphasized—this kind of situation could also help a teacher identify those particular children who have difficulty even in remembering a word that is as personal as their own name.

Another safe assumption about kindergartens today is that art activities continue to be a part of the curriculum. Without diminishing their value as forms of free expression, finished products in art provide a most opportune time to offer kindergarten children the chance to learn to sign their names, to write their own captions, and to read those composed by others. At the same time, however, the same situation is the teacher's opportunity to identify children whose way into beginning reading might be through writing and spelling; to identify those who remember whole words with a minimum of exposure to them; but also to become aware of children for whom the motor skill of writing is a formidable task, or for whom it is very difficult to compose even the briefest of captions.

Another activity that is to be found in kindergartens is that of reading to the children. Generally this is done for enjoyment or perhaps for gathering information to answer questions that were raised when magnets were being discussed or when conflicting ideas appeared in a spontaneous conversation about the stars being out at night but not in the day time. Periodically, as part of this reading, the kindergarten teacher might write a word like *magnet* on the chalkboard, identify it, and then ask, "Does anybody know the name of this first letter?" or, "Does anybody have a name that starts with this same letter?" or—after *Marcy, Michael,* and *Matthew* have been written—"I'm going to say all of these words to show you that they not only begin with the same letter but also with the same sound." And then later, "Can you think of other words that begin with the same sound as *magnet*?" Obviously with this kind of questioning—proposed here as an informal evaluative technique—a kindergarten teacher can identify children who seem to know the alphabet as well as those who have skill in making visual and auditory discriminations. But, too, she is becoming aware of other children who appear to have no acquaintance even with a few letters of the alphabet or, more likely, no understanding of what is meant by the description "begin with the same sound."

Perhaps these few illustrations of very ordinary kindergarten activities are sufficient to give specific meaning to what I have recommended as a valid way of assessing a child's readiness to read. Implied even in these few illustrations, however, are some basic assumptions about readiness and beginning reading which seem important enough to merit explicit attention.

Assumptions Inherent in Recommendation

One obvious and important assumption underlying the illustrations is that the assessment of readiness and the teaching of beginning reading can result from the same situation. For instance, the teacher's use of written names in attendance-taking was proposed as a way of collecting some diagnostic information about the readiness of the children; but, in addition, for the individual children who were in fact "ready" it could be the start of learning to read—in this instance, learning to read children's names.

A second assumption that ought to be made explicit is that the same situation serves for readiness instruction and also for instruction in beginning reading. For example, the use that was made of the word *magnet* in one of the illustrations could result in beginning learnings in phonics for some children. For other less ready children, however, the teacher's questions about a particular group of words would only be the first step in a series of steps which will finally result in their understanding that some words "sound the same at the beginning." With these latter children, the kindergarten teacher was carrying on readiness instruction. Yet, with other children who were ready to grasp the association between the letter *m* and a certain sound, reading instruction was taking place.

To combine into one situation—as these illustrations do—instances of readiness assessment, readiness instruction, and beginning reading instruction is, of course, to go contrary to the more traditional viewpoint. Traditionally, the readiness program and the reading program have been separated, both in time and in the minds of many teachers. However, it would seem that this separation is no longer defensible, if it can be assumed that there really is no absolute demarcation between readiness learnings and beginning learnings in reading. It is on just such an assumption that I have been suggesting that the readiness of children to read can be assessed most accurately by giving them varied opportunities to begin.

Problems Related to Recommendation

Promoting this way of assessing readiness is not necessarily forgetting the problems of putting it into practice. In one sense the problem of greatest significance is that the recommendation allows for a situation which could put us right back to the 1920's and 1930's in our basic conception of readiness. More specifically, if the learning opportunities offered to children turn out to be uninteresting, routine, and, therefore, not at all productive of some achievements related to reading, then there is the temptation to conclude —as happened on a very wide scale back in the 1920's and the 1930's—that the children did not learn because they were not ready. What this suggests is that in any situation in which readiness is being assessed in relation to a response to learning opportunities, careful attention must always be given to the quality of these opportunities. Otherwise it becomes impossible to judge whether the shortcomings lay with the child or with the kind of instruction that was available.

There are, to be sure, still other very practical difficulties connected with this way of assessing readiness. For instance, matters like finding sufficient time and, too, finding ways to keep an account of what and how much is being learned by individual children are very real problems, especially at the kindergarten level. I say "especially" because as kindergartens are now conceived there is hardly enough time in a day to delve into anything very deeply. However, if and when the whole of the kindergarten program is revamped so as to reflect five-year-olds of today rather than those of years gone by, it would be very safe to conjecture that the new kindergarten day would be longer and the classes smaller. With such reform it then would be realistic to hope that very valuable diagnostic information could be collected on each kindergarten child. This hope would have even a greater chance of being realized, however, if more careful and systematic attention were given to informal evaluative techniques at the beginning stages of reading.

REFERENCES

1. Arthur, Grace. "A Quantitative Study of the Results of Grouping First Grade Children According to Mental Age," *Journal of Educational Research, 12* (October, 1925), 173-185.
2. Ausubel, David P. "Viewpoints from Related Disciplines: Human Growth and Development," *Teachers College Record, 60* (February, 1959), 245-254.
3. Bloom, Benjamin S. *Stability and Change in Human Characteristics*. New York: John Wiley and Sons, 1964.
4. Durkin, Dolores. *Children Who Read Early*. New York: Teachers College Press, Columbia University, 1966.
5. Dykstra, Robert. "Auditory Discrimination: Abilities and Beginning Reading Achievement," *Reading Research Quarterly, 1* (Spring, 1966), 5-34.
6. Harrison, M. Lucille. *Reading Readiness*. Boston: Houghton Mifflin Company, 1936.
7. Holmes, Margaret C. "Investigation of Reading Readiness of First Grade Entrants," *Childhood Education, 3* (January, 1927), 215-221.
8. Hunt, J. McVicker. *Intelligence and Experience*. New York: The Ronald Press Co., 1961.
9. Zornow, T. A., and L. A. Pechstein. "An Experiment in the Classification of First-Grade Children Through the Use of Mental Tests," *Elementary School Journal, 23* (October, 1922), 136-146.

Robert Dykstra

UNIVERSITY OF MINNESOTA

4. The Use of Reading Readiness Tests for Prediction and Diagnosis: A Critique

THERE IS GENERAL AGREEMENT today that reading readiness is a vital aspect of the beginning reading program. Many people feel that a child's success in learning to read depends to a great extent upon whether the child was ready when he began formal reading activities. Since reading readiness is such an important part of the reading program, determining the readiness of each child is an essential element of the beginning reading program. Reading readiness tests are frequently considered as an aid in determining each child's readiness to read. Austin and Morrison (2) found that more than 80 percent of the schools contacted nationally reported the use of reading readiness tests for prereading evaluation.

An examination of reading readiness test manuals reveals that the typical reading readiness test has two purposes: the identification of pupils who are ready to read and the diagnosis of an individual child's deficiencies in skills considered prerequisite to success in reading. Test authors, however, in their suggestions to teachers regarding the use of the tests, differ a great deal in the emphases given the two functions. It is the purpose of this paper, therefore, to cast new light on the role of reading readiness tests in diagnosis and prediction by reexamining pertinent research in the area.

Research on the Readiness Approach to Reading

In the last thirty-five years a great deal of research has been conducted in the general area of reading readiness. This research has been concerned primarily with identifying the factors most highly related to success in beginning reading, and with assessing the degree of relationship between various prereading characteristics and success in initial reading instruction. Let us now examine the research and suggest implications regarding the use of reading readiness tests for diagnosis and prediction.

A teacher's use of readiness tests is predicated on most, if not all, of the following assumptions: (a) a readiness test can measure reliably what it proposes to measure, (b) the skills tested by a readiness battery are related to success in beginning reading, (c) readiness tests serve a unique function in regard to predicting a child's success in learning how to read, (d) pupils who score poorly on a reading readiness test would be better off with readiness training than with formal reading instruction, and (e) readiness for reading can be developed through training.

Assumption number one: readiness can be measured. An obvious first assumption which must be made by the user of reading readiness tests is that these tests measure reliably those skills which they purport to measure. An examination of reading readiness test manuals indicates that in general the reading readiness test is a reliable instrument. Reliability coefficients based on the total score of the test often reach .90 or better.

Reliability data on subtest scores are less common and also less encouraging. As one might expect, those tests which do report reliability on subtests show these reliabilities to be considerably lower than total test reliability. One widely used readiness test reports reliability coefficients of .50, .33, and .33 for one of its subtests based on three separate samples of pupils (*16*). This same reading readiness test reports intercorrelations of this subtest with other subtests in the battery ranging from .36 to .50. The reliability of this subtest is unusually low compared to the reliability of the other subtests in the battery, but it does point up a basic problem. The diagnostic use of readiness tests is a very questionable practice when a subtest correlates as well or better with another subtest in the battery as it does with itself. Incidentally, it should be pointed out that the readiness test in question discourages analysis of subtest scores. It appears to me that tests which encourage diagnosis of weaknesses on the basis of a profile of subtest scores should first of all produce evidence that these subtests are in fact reliable measures of the skills tested.

A related problem is the question of whether or not readiness tests measure the skills they set out to measure. Many readiness tests stress the content validity of their instruments. The authors first list the prereading skills and capabilities which they consider essential to success in reading and then set up tests to measure these skills. Other test authors stress the predictive validity of their tests. Information concerning predictive validity will be discussed later.

There is some reason to believe that perhaps some readiness tests do not, in fact, measure what they purport to measure. For example, a study by Dykstra (*9*) revealed intercorrelations of less than .35 between measures of auditory discrimination from three reading readiness batteries. Obviously these three subtests, all of which were designed to measure auditory discrimination, appeared not to be measuring the same skill.

Assumption number two: skills tested by readiness tests are related to success in reading. Information concerning this assumption can be gathered in a number of ways. This discussion will center on three. Research will be reviewed which deals with (a) correlation studies of the relationship between total readiness batteries and subsequent reading success, (b) correlation studies of the relationship between various skills measured by subtests and subsequent reading success, and (c) noncorrelational studies which compare a pupil's end-of-first-grade reading achievement with his expected achievement based on readiness test results.

During the past thirty years many studies have been published to demonstrate the predictive validity of reading readiness tests. These studies have in common the administration of a reading readiness test at the end of kindergarten or, more commonly, during the first weeks of the first grade and a reading achievement test at the end of the first grade. The relationship between pupils' performance on these two measures is then evaluated by means of a correlation analysis. The results of a number of such investigations are reported in *Table 1*. The studies reported range over a period of thirty years and are based on a variety of readiness tests, and on a number of revisions of the same test. Furthermore, the studies utilize a variety of sample sizes and use a number of different reading achievement measures. Despite this fact, predictive validity correlation coefficients are in general quite consistent. Most of the relationships can be found in the range from .40 to .60 with a few extremes on either end. The median correlation between total readiness score and first grade reading achievement as reported by the studies in *Table 1* is .55. This is a significant relationship from a statistical point of view and does demonstrate the predictive validity of reading readiness tests.

There have also been many studies conducted to investigate the relationship of various reading readiness subtest skills to subsequent success in learning how to read. The skills usually evaluated are letter knowledge, visual discrimination, and auditory discrimination. Rather than tabulating the results of the many individual studies of this nature conducted during the past thirty years, correlational relationships will be reported based on the data from the Cooperative Research Study in First Grade Reading Instruction which was coordinated at the University of Minnesota (Cooperative Research Project X-001). The correlation coefficients are based on a total sample of 4,266 pupils enrolled in 187 basal reader classes from seventeen projects. The best single subtest predictor of achievement on the Stanford Paragraph Meaning Test was the Murphy-Durrell Letter Names Subtest, which correlated .52 with the criterion. Correlations with the Stanford Paragraph Meaning Test of .46, .40, .34, .29, .30, and .23 were reported for the Murphy-Durrell Phonemes Subtest, Murphy-Durrell Learning Rate Subtest, Thurstone Pattern Copying Test, Thurstone-Jeffrey

TABLE I
Predictive Validity Studies of Reading Readiness Tests

Study*	Readiness Test	Reading Test	Number of Cases	Coefficient of Correlation
Banham (3)	S.R.A.	Metropolitan	71	.69
Bremer (5)	Metropolitan	Gray-Votaw-Rogers	2069	.40
Dean (7)	Metropolitan	Metropolitan	116	.59
	Monroe			.41
Fry (12)	Metropolitan	Stanford Paragraph Meaning	393	.62
Hayes (14)	Metropolitan	Stanford Paragraph Reading	363	.64
	Lee-Clark			.55
Karlin (17)	Metropolitan	Gates Primary	111	.36
Kottmeyer (19)	Metropolitan	Gates (avg. of WR & PM)	3115	.46
Lee, Clark, Lee (21)	Lee-Clark	Lee-Clark Primary Test	164	.49
Powell & Parsley (29)	Lee-Clark	California Reading Comprehension	703	.43
Sheldon (32)	Metropolitan	Stanford Paragraph Meaning	467	.70
Stauffer (36)	Metropolitan	Stanford Paragraph Meaning	201 (Basal)**	.47
			232 (Language Experience)**	.78
Tanyzer (37)	Metropolitan	Stanford Paragraph Meaning	220 (Lippincott)**	.52
			220 (Scott-Foresman)**	.57
			220 (ITA)**	.62
Thackray (38)	Harrison-Stroud	Southgate Reading Test	182	.59
Wright (39)	Metropolitan	Gates	208	.44

* Number in parenthesis refers to bibliographic reference.
** Correlations were computed separately for various treatment groups.

Identical Forms, Metropolitan Word Meaning Subtest, and Metropolitan Listening Subtest. All of the obtained correlations were statistically significant indicating that the prereading skills are related to subsequent achievement. It is interesting to note that the correlation of .52 between the Letter Names Subtest and reading achievement is of approximately the same magnitude as the median correlation presented earlier between total readiness batteries and reading achievement. In a recent multiple regression analysis of the relationship between a variety of prereading measures (auditory discrimination, visual discrimination, mental age, socioeconomic status, etc.) and first grade reading achievement the investigator concluded, "It appears that the single factor of letter identification can be used to predict reading achievement as well as all or any combinations of the readiness factors used in the present study" (34).

The question arises as to the practical significance of a correlation coefficient in the range of .50 to .60. Although the relationships reported are statistically significant, how meaningful are they in a practical sense? One way to assess their significance would be in terms of the coefficient of alienation which indicates the size of the error in predicting an individual score relative to the error which would result from a mere guess. It is somewhat discouraging to note that a predictive validity coefficient of .60 yields an error of estimate which is 80 percent as large as would be expected from merely guessing a pupil's reading achievement scores. However, this interpretation is somewhat misleading. The first grade teacher is not primarily interested in predicting a specific reading score for each of her pupils. She *is* interested in making a rather general prediction about the extent to which the child can profit from formal reading instruction. From this point of view pupils who score well on a readiness test given at the beginning of first grade should in general be the best readers at the end of the first grade, and pupils scoring poorly on the readiness test should be achieving at a lower level in reading at the end of the first grade. A relatively small number of studies investigates this situation.

Fendrick and McGlade (11) identified 17 pupils out of 66 whose scores on the Metropolitan Readiness Test indicated that they would be unable to make satisfactory progress in first grade school work. However, of the 17 potential low achievers, 8 made satisfactory progress according to the criteria set up in advance. In addition, out of 49 cases whose prognosis was satisfactory reading achievement based on the readiness score, 45 pupils did satisfy the criterion. This study indicates then that in general those pupils who score well on a readiness test do in fact learn to read well. Prediction is less valid for pupils who score poorly on the readiness test.

Bremer (5) classified pupils as low, average, or high in readiness on the basis of their performance on the Metropolitan Readiness Test and then classified the same pupils from low to high in reading achievement at the end of the first grade. Among his findings he reports that approximately one-third of his low readiness group made reading test scores that fell in the lowest level of reading achievement. However, approximately another one-third of his low readiness group scored above average in the reading achievement test at the end of the first grade. Of the high readiness group about 35 percent had reading test scores in the highest level, but about 26 percent had scores that were below average. Here again the prediction of reading success for individual pupils proved to be a hazardous task.

A recent extensive study by Spache (*35*) yields further information. In this study expectancy tables were developed to predict end-of-first-grade Stanford Achievement Reading scores based on six measures of reading readiness. Individual expectancy tables were developed for each of four experimental groups and the investigator concluded, "These tables, each being based on the best combination of predictor variables, afford the teacher little assistance in predicting end-of-year reading achievement on the basis of September performance on tests in this battery."

Assumption number three: skills measured by reading readiness tests are uniquely related to reading achievement. Another assumption made by users of readiness tests is that the readiness test has a unique contribution to make to the prediction of reading success. The readiness test is better for this purpose than would be, for example, an intelligence test. Many reading authorities suggest that readiness tests should be given in addition to such evaluative measures as intelligence tests, teacher judgment, and physical examinations. One way to check this assumption would be to compare the predictive validity of readiness tests with the predictive validity of various other kinds of measures. In a study of this nature Dean (*7*) found Stanford-Binet mental age to be more highly related to reading success than either of two measures of reading readiness. Studies by Fry (*12*), Hayes (*14*), Sheldon (*32*), Stauffer (*36*), and Tanyzer (*37*) report correlations between the Pintner-Cunningham Intelligence Test and Stanford Reading Achievement of .75, .63, .59, .43, and .49. (Correlations reported for Stauffer and Tanyzer are based on basal reader treatment only.) These correlations compare favorably with the correlations between readiness and reading obtained in the same investigations reported on *Table I*. In addition, Thackray (*38*) found a correlation of .44 between the Kelvin Measure of Ability Test and subsequent reading achievement as compared to a correlation of .42 between a reading readiness test and the same criterion. Wright (*39*) found a correlation of .55 between intelligence test results and end-of-first-grade reading results. This correlation was considerably higher than that reported in the same investigation between a reading readiness test and end-of-first-grade reading achievement. Therefore, it appears that when intelligence tests and reading readiness tests are used in the same investigations to predict reading achievement, little if any difference can be found between them in their predictive validity.

Other instruments, not specifically designed to measure reading readiness factors, also have been found to correlate quite highly with subsequent reading achievement. For example, the group Bender-Gestalt, when administered at the end of the kindergarten year, correlated .50 with reading achievement measured at the end of the first grade (18). The Rorschach Test, when administered in kindergarten, correlated .53 with reading achievement in the fifth grade (1). In still another study (10) a predictive validity correlation of .64 was found between the Draw-A-Man Test administered in kindergarten and reading achievement at the end of the first grade. It is also interesting to note the extent to which first grade reading ability is related to general knowledge of numbers at the beginning of first grade. The Metropolitan Readiness Test has a subtest entitled Numbers which is described as "an inventory of the child's stock of number concepts, number knowledge, ability to manipulate quantitative relationships, recognition of and ability to produce number symbols, and related knowledge, such as concepts of money (16)." The test authors state that "the Numbers test has repeatedly been shown to be the single most powerful predictive subtest of the earlier forms of the Metropolitan Readiness Tests." Corroborative data concerning this statement can be found in four recent studies in which correlations between the Numbers subtest and the Stanford Paragraph Meaning Test were found to be .55(14); .66(32); .71 for a language experience group, .46 for a basal group, and .43, .58, and .46 for a Lippincott group, an i.t.a. group, and a basal group (36, 37). It is apparent from these investigations that many other evaluative measures, not specifically designed to test reading readiness, predict reading achievement just about as well as do readiness tests.

Another way to assess the unique contribution of readiness tests is to compare prediction based on test scores with prediction based on teacher estimates. Henig (15) found "first grade teachers were just as successful in predicting the degree of success their charges would meet in learning to read as was the standardized reading readiness test." It should be pointed out that success was measured in this study in terms of teachers' marks so the results should be interpreted with caution. Carr and Michaels (6) reported a mean rank order correlation of .79 between ratings of readiness assigned early in the year by the teacher and the rank on a criterion of success in reading near the end of the year. This reported correlation is the average correlation between teacher ranking and reading achievement from fourteen classrooms. One might question the advisability of averaging correlation coefficients but it is impossible to downgrade the substantial nature of the correlations obtained. Teachers, after spending a few weeks with a group of children, can predict quite well how successful each pupil will be in learning to read.

Numerous studies have also indicated the high correlation between readiness tests and various other measures. It would appear that if a readiness test is to make a unique contribution to assessing the child's readiness for reading it should correlate to a relatively minor degree with other prognostic instruments. However, in four recent studies correlations can be found between the Pintner-Cunningham Intelligence Test and the Metropolitan Readiness Test of .56 (*12*), .78 (*14*), .73 (*32*), and .64 (*37*). Another study (*7*) found the almost unbelievable product-moment correlation of .94 between scores on the Detroit First Grade Intelligence Test and those on the Metropolitan Readiness Test. It is apparent that pupils who score well on the Metropolitan Readiness Test also score well on certain group tests of intelligence. In many cases it may be difficult to point up the differences between primary grade group intelligence tests and first grade reading readiness tests.

Assumption number four: pupils who score low on a readiness test will be better off with readiness training than with formal reading instruction. The user of readiness tests assumes that pupils who score poorly are not likely to profit from formal reading instruction and should pursue additional readiness activities. A related assumption is that these immature pupils will profit more from additional readiness training than from formal reading instruction. A number of problems frustrate research in this area. For one thing, it is probably somewhat unfair to compare at the end of one year reading achievement of a group which has received reading instruction for nine months with another group of pupils who have spent less time in actual reading instruction. Perhaps the effects of the additional readiness training would not be apparent until after two or three years of instruction. However, since the assumption listed would appear to be one which should be investigated, some of the pertinent research will be examined.

Relatively few studies bear directly on this question. A study by Bradley (*4*) compared the reading achievement at the end of the second grade and at the end of the third grade of two classrooms of first grade children. The experimental group participated in a program which was built on the concept of readiness, and formal systematic instruction in reading was not given until the child was considered ready. As a result, formal reading instruction was delayed for some pupils for many months. The control group began reading instruction almost immediately upon entering the first grade. Results showed the control group (the reading instruction group) to be significantly superior in November of the second grade. No differences were found between the two groups at the end of the second and third grades.

Orme (27) compared the reading achievement after one year of instruction between two groups, one which had a diagnostic readiness approach and another which initiated formal reading instruction almost immediately. The investigator reports that at the end of the first year the scores of the children in the readiness group were above those of the control group. However, no statistical analysis was reported. Mann (23) found that near the end of the first grade, immature pupils in a traditional program were significantly superior in paragraph reading to an experimental group of immature pupils who had had an extended reading readiness program. A study of a somewhat different nature (24) found a one- to three-week readiness period to be just as effective as a seven- to eleven-week readiness period in terms of first grade reading achievement. A recent comprehensive study (35) provided the best information yet on this question. This study was designed to assess the effectiveness of an extended readiness program for low readiness pupils. An experimental group was administered a battery of reading readiness tests and all those pupils scoring below a specified cutoff were given specialized training to develop their specific weaknesses. The control group was given the traditional few weeks of readiness training after which pupils started formal reading instruction. Results indicated no differences between the experimental and control groups in reading achievement after one year of instruction, except in the case of Negro boys. The readiness program was superior for this group.

It is difficult to draw any conclusions about this fourth assumption because of the paucity of research. However, there is some indication that no differences exist in reading achievement after one year between pupils who follow a *readiness approach* to reading and pupils who follow a more traditional primary reading program. This finding could be interpreted two ways. On the one hand, if children can do as well on a reading test at the end of the first grade even though they have had a shorter period of formal reading instruction, this may be a point in favor of the readiness approach. On the other hand, if there is no evidence that children do any better by pursuing a lengthy readiness program perhaps they could just as well begin formal reading instruction.

Assumption number five: readiness skills can be developed through training.
If a teacher is to use readiness tests diagnostically, and if she considers readiness an educational concept (rather than a maturational one), she must assume that areas of weakness pointed out by the readiness test profile can be improved through instruction. The study by Spache (35) casts some light on the tenability of this hypothesis. As was indicated earlier, this study assessed the effectiveness of an extended reading readiness program in which lessons were planned to alleviate specific weaknesses in reading readiness. A battery of reading readiness tests was administered in September, November, January, and March. Pupils falling below specified cutoff

points in visual discrimination, auditory discrimination, and auditory language abilities were given specialized instruction to alleviate these difficulties. Their progress in these readiness abilities was then compared with a control group which followed a typical basal reader program with a characteristic short period of readiness instruction at the beginning of the year. The control group took the same tests at the same time as did the experimental group, but the results of the tests were not made known to the participating teachers and pupils.

The effectiveness of training was evaluated separately for boys and girls, for Negro and white subjects, and for pupils with varying degrees of intelligence. Therefore, only a general statement will be made concerning the extent to which specialized instruction affects visual discrimination, auditory discrimination, and language facility. Furthermore, because of space limitations, this discussion will focus on the measured reading readiness skills of the experimental and control groups at the time of the November testing. Eight weeks of concentrated instruction on a basic readiness ability should bring about changes if the skill in question is amenable to specialized instruction.

In general, specialized training in visual discrimination seemed to improve performance on the Thurstone Pattern Copying Test beyond that achieved by the control group, but did not have a similar effect on the Thurstone-Jeffrey Identical Forms Test. At the November testing only one significant difference between experimental and control groups was found on the Identical Forms Test, and this difference favored *control* Negro girls. Two measures of auditory discrimination were also administered at the various testing times. When the experimental and control groups were administered tests of auditory discrimination in November no differences were found. The control or basal reader group improved its auditory discrimination abilities at the same rate as did the group given specialized training in these skills.

A readiness factor identified as facility in language was measured by the Word Meaning and Listening subtests of the Metropolitan Readiness Test. In general the November administration of the Word Meaning test indicated no differences between the experimental and control groups. Performance on the Listening subtest was less consistent. No differences were found between experimental and control groups composed of Negro subjects, but significant differences favoring the experimental treatment were found for white subjects.

Drawing conclusions from the study just reported is by no means an easy task. However, the evidence appears to indicate clearly that specialized readiness training will not necessarily lead to significantly greater improvement in the skills identified in this study. In many cases a more traditional primary reading approach with a short period of general readiness training and an early introduction to formal reading instruction improves readiness skills to the same extent. However, it must be pointed out again that performance was compared only on the readiness measures during the November testing period. Different conclusions might have been drawn from an examination of the January or March test results.

Other studies are also pertinent to this discussion. Rosen (30) found that 29 one-half hour training sessions designed to improve visual perception of beginning first grade pupils led to significantly superior performance on the Frostig Developmental Tests of Visual Perception over that attained by a control group. Mann (23) evaluated the effectiveness of an extended reading readiness program for immature pupils in the first grade. The extended readiness group was involved in 74 specialized readiness lessons. Performance of this experimental group was compared at midsemester and at the end of the semester with the performance of a control group. No differences in readiness skills were found between the groups at either testing period. A related question concerns the use of reading readiness workbooks. The question might be raised as to the extent to which these workbooks promote reading readiness. Ploghoft (28) compared the reading readiness test scores of pupils who had utilized readiness workbooks during the last nine weeks of kindergarten with the scores of pupils who had not used such materials. No differences in readiness, as measured by the tests at the beginning of first grade, were found. In a similar study Silberberg (33) compared readiness test scores of two groups of pupils, one of which followed an informal kindergarten program, and one which followed a formal reading readiness program during the last eight weeks of kindergarten. Readiness test performance, which immediately followed the experimental period, indicated no differences in measured readiness. However, this same investigation found significant differences in favor of the experimental group on the same readiness test which was administered three weeks after the beginning of school the following fall.

On the other hand, Rutherford (31) found that a program of sensory-motor and ocular training during a daily thirty minute outdoor play period led to significantly superior performance on the Metropolitan Readiness Test over that of a control group of children who did not receive such training. It is interesting to note that this more generalized type of training led to readiness test performance which was significantly better than the performance of a control group while more specific reading-related types of readiness instruction in a majority of cases produced readiness test performance no better than that achieved by a control group.

Summary and Recommendations

The research reviewed in this presentation can be summarized in a number of statements.
1. The readiness test as a whole is a reliable instrument. However, there is a question as to whether or not subtests of readiness batteries are sufficiently reliable to permit the teacher to make a differential diagnosis of the child's prereading capabilities.
2. Performance on readiness test batteries as well as on subtests within these batteries is significantly related to subsequent reading achievement. Correlation coefficients for readiness batteries as well as for individual subtests generally range from .40 to .70, with relatively few of them reaching the upper limits of this range. As a general rule, prediction of reading success can be made almost as accurately by using a single subtest (such as letter recognition) as by employing an entire readiness test battery. Nevertheless, prediction of an individual's achievement at the end of the first grade is very difficult.
3. A number of evaluation techniques predict first grade reading achievement just about as well as do reading readiness tests. The predictive validity of primary group intelligence tests, for example, is not substantially different from the predictive validity of readiness tests. Furthermore, ability to deal with numbers is related to success in first grade reading to almost the same extent. There is little evidence to indicate that the readiness test makes a *unique* contribution to a prognosis of the child's capability to profit from reading instruction.
4. Research evidence does not substantiate the claim that immature pupils profit more from readiness instruction than from formal reading instruction. However, most studies which have investigated this area of primary reading instruction have been concerned only with progress at the end of first grade and therefore the statement made is generalizable only to this phase of the total school program. Perhaps an extended readiness program for immature pupils would pay off in the long run, but evidence of this is lacking.
5. Research is in general agreement that skills measured by readiness tests are developmental in nature. As children progress through the first grade they improve their language facility, visual discrimination, and auditory discrimination. However, it is indicated that some of these abilities develop as rapidly as a result of formal reading instruction as they do in a diagnostic readiness program. Likewise, there is no clear-cut evidence that the use of readiness workbooks and readiness materials improves a child's readiness for reading beyond what could be expected from an informal kindergarten program.

Implications for Instruction

In light of the research reviewed what implications can be drawn? Generally, there appears to be little reason for administering a complete readiness battery if the only reason for its administration is the classification of pupils and the determination for each of when to initiate reading instruction. A recent study (8) indicates this to be the primary use made by teachers of readiness test results. In the usual situation, it seems that decisions regarding the initiation of reading instruction can be made without administering a complete readiness test battery and that the time usually spent in the administration and scoring of readiness tests can better be utilized for instruction. In the first place an experienced teacher, after a few weeks with the class, can probably assign children quite adequately to instructional groups. Furthermore, the administration of a simple letter recognition test or a number knowledge test can assign pupils to the bluebird, blackbird, or robin reading group with almost the same degree of confidence as can be gained from a total readiness test score. Then, too, since today the kindergarten is becoming an integral part of the American educational program, valid information about the child's readiness for reading instruction can be obtained from the kindergarten teacher. She will probably know a great deal about the child's interest in reading, ability to learn, emotional readiness, and other factors which are very important and yet often are not measured by the typical readiness test. In addition, if an intelligence test is given routinely as a part of the school testing program, there is little reason for also giving a reading readiness test. This is in no way meant to reflect negatively on the validity of readiness tests, since they do possess predictive validity. Nevertheless, the opinion that in the normal school situation a readiness test may not be an essential measure for determining when to begin reading instruction seems to be defensible.

A close look will now be taken at the recommendation that, if a test is given, it be a letter recognition test. Why not some other test? Although any number of readiness subtests might be used, there are a number of reasons that a test of letter knowledge might be particularly valuable as an indicator of a child's readiness for reading. In the first place, it is relatively easy to administer and can be administered at the same time to a group of children. Letter knowledge can also be measured reliably as evidenced by the relatively high subtest reliabilities reported for this measure in readiness test batteries. Scoring is a simple matter. Then, too, research shows letter knowledge to be the single best predictor of first grade reading success, and prediction can be made almost as accurately on the basis of this one simple test as with an entire readiness battery.

There are some reasonable explanations for the effectiveness of letter knowledge as a predictor of reading achievement. Words are made up of letters, so there is some logic in assuming that a child who can recognize letters may be more adept at learning to recognize words. In addition, letter knowledge undoubtedly reflects home background, suggesting that the child who can recognize letters when he comes to school has probably had more background with books and other reading materials. Furthermore, the child who has learned the letters has demonstrated that he can in fact learn; this is in a sense a crude measure of the child's intelligence. Then, too, the child who demonstrates letter knowledge also demonstrates visual and auditory discrimination. A pupil who can pick out a *b* from a row of letters including a *p* and a *d* demonstrates that he can make visual discriminations. Likewise the child who can circle the letter *b* when given a verbal command to do so must be able to hear the difference between the names for such similar sounding letters as *d* and *p*. Therefore, it seems that a letter knowledge test measures many skills and understandings which have been found to be related to success in reading. In some respects we might say that a test of letter recognition measures to some degree the major characteristics evaluated in a typical reading readiness test.

Perhaps a final word should be said about the use of reading readiness tests for diagnostic purposes. It seems clear that the majority of readiness tests should be used for differential diagnosis. In the first place, not all readiness test authors report reliability data for battery subtests. In the absence of such data a diagnostic profile must be considered to be of questionable value. Furthermore, two well-known tests which do report subtest reliabilities tend to discourage the diagnostic use of test results. One manual (*20*) says, "The Lee-Clark Reading Readiness Test is designed to provide the teacher with an objective basis for identifying children who are ready to receive reading instruction." The Metropolitan Readiness Test Manual (*16*) advises that "efforts to attach significance to the subtest scores of individual pupils are not encouraged." Many subtests are too short to be reliable; moreover, when administered in a group situation, they often appear to measure a general test-taking ability or general ability to follow directions rather than a more specific skill. If tests are to be used diagnostically, test makers should demonstrate that subtests within the battery do in fact measure the fairly specific skill they claim to measure. In order to do this, validity of a different nature from predictive validity will have to be proven.

One more point should be made in this regard. If a subtest has been demonstrated to measure reliably such subskills as auditory discrimination and visual discrimination, pupils scoring very poorly in a given skill should be given supplementary training in that skill along with the initial stages of actual reading instruction. There is little in the research which indicates that delaying reading instruction is necessarily helpful. On the other hand it may well be that initiating reading instruction, pacing the instruction according to the capability of the youngster, and giving additional training in skills in which he is deficient may prove to be of value. This recommendation, as all others, of course, is not expected to hold in all situations and must be tempered by the good judgment of a well-prepared teacher.

Finally, if an inexperienced teacher wishes to use a readiness test to help in classifying pupils, she should be encouraged to use one. She may well need the assurance of an objective measure to reinforce her judgments about individual children. If an experienced teacher has found readiness tests to be helpful in her classification of children, she should by all means be encouraged to use them also. After all, readiness tests do predict subsequent reading success. However, the widespread use of readiness tests for prediction is not essential and may be an inefficient use of the teacher's time. Also, the use of the majority of current readiness tests for diagnosis is based primarily on intuition and is not warranted by available evidence. It is time to reexamine readiness tests themselves and also time to reexamine the purposes for which they are used.

REFERENCES

1. Ames, Louise B., and Richard N. Walker. "Prediction of Later Reading Ability from Kindergarten Rorschach and I.Q. Scores," *Journal of Educational Psychology*, 55 (Dec. 1964), 309-13.
2. Austin, Mary C., and Coleman Morrison. *The First R: The Harvard Report on Reading in Elementary Schools.* New York: MacMillan, 1963, 19-20.
3. Banham, Katharine M. "Maturity Level for Reading-Readiness," *Educational and Psychological Measurement*, 18 (Summer 1958), 371-75.
4. Bradley, Beatrice E. "An Experimental Study of the Readiness Approach to Reading," *Elementary School Journal*, 56 (Feb. 1956), 262-67.
5. Bremer, Neville. "Do Readiness Tests Predict Success in Reading?" *Elementary School Journal*, 59 (Jan. 1959), 222-24.
6. Carr, John W., Jr., and Matilda O. Michaels. "Reading Readiness Tests and Grouping of First Grade Entrants," *Elementary English Review*, 18 (April 1941), 133-38.
7. Dean, Charles D. "Predicting First-Grade Reading Achievement," *Elementary School Journal*, 39 (April 1939), 609-16.
8. Dunn, June Markgraf. "A Study of the Role of Reading Readiness Tests," unpublished master's paper, University of Minnesota, 1965.
9. Dykstra, Robert. "Auditory Discrimination and Beginning Reading Achievement," *Reading Research Quarterly*, 1 (Spring 1966), 5-34.
10. Easley, Glenn Truett. "The Draw-A-Man Tests as Index of Reading Readiness," *Dissertation Abstracts*, 25 (Nov. 1964), p. 2281.
11. Fendrick, Paul, and Charles A. McGlade. "A Validation of Two Prognostic

Tests of Reading Aptitude," *Elementary School Journal*, *39* (Nov. 1938), 187-94.
12. Fry, Edward Bernard. *First Grade Reading Instruction Using a Diacritical Marking System, The Initial Teaching Alphabet and a Basal Reading System* (USOE Cooperative Research Project No. 2745). New Brunswick, New Jersey: Rutgers, The State University, 1965.
13. Harrison, M. Lucile, and James B. Stroud. *The Harrison-Stroud Reading Readiness Profiles*. Boston: Houghton-Mifflin, 1950, 1956.
14. Hayes, Robert B., and Joseph S. Nemeth. *An Attempt to Secure Additional Evidence Concerning Factors Affecting Learning to Read* (USOE Cooperative Research Project No. 2697). Harrisburg, Pennsylvania: Pennsylvania Department of Education, 1965.
15. Henig, Max S. "Predictive Value of a Reading-Readiness Test and of Teacher's Forecasts," *Elementary School Journal*, *50* (Sept. 1949), 41-46.
16. Hildreth, Gertrude H., Nellie L. Griffiths, and Mary E. McGauvran. *Metropolitan Readiness Tests*. New York: Harcourt, Brace and World, 1964.
17. Karlin, Robert. "The Prediction of Reading Success and Reading-Readiness Tests," *Elementary English*, *34* (May 1957), 320-22.
18. Keogh, Barbara K. "The Bender-Gestalt as a Predictive and Diagnostic Test of Reading Performance," *Dissertation Abstracts*, *24* (Dec. 1963) 2360.
19. Kottmeyer, William. "Readiness for Reading," *Elementary English*, *24* (Oct. 1947). 355-66.
20. Lee, J. Murray, and Willis W. Clark. *Lee-Clark Reading Readiness Test* (1962 Revision). Monterey, California: California Test Bureau, 1962.
21. Lee, J. Murray, W. W. Clark, and D. M. Lee. "Measuring Reading Readiness," *Elementary School Journal*, *34* (May 1934), 656-66.
22. Linehan, Eleanor B. "Early Instruction in Letter Names and Sounds as Related to Success in Beginning Reading," *Journal of Education*, *140* (Feb. 1958), 44-88.
23. Mann, Leta M. "An Extended Reading Readiness Program for a Selected Group in the First Grade," *Dissertation Abstracts*, *22* (Nov. 1966), 1521.
24. Miller, Grover C. "The Effect of an Experimental Approach to Promoting Reading Readiness on Certain Aspects of Reading Achievement at the First Grade Level," *Dissertation Abstracts*, *25* (1964), 1788-89.
25. Murphy, Helen A., and Donald D. Durrell. *Murphy-Durrell Diagnostic Reading Readiness Test* (rev. ed.). New York: Harcourt, Brace, and World, 1964.
26. Olson, Arthur V. "Growth in Word Perception Abilities as it Relates to Success in Beginning Reading," *Journal of Education*, *140* (Feb. 1958), 35-36.
27. Orme, Lillian. "Building Readiness for Reading in First-Grade Children Through Special Instructions," Albert J. Harris, (Ed.), *Readings on Reading Instruction*. New York: David McKay, 1963, pp. 83-86.
28. Ploghoft, Milton H. "Do Reading Readiness Workbooks Promote Readiness," *Elementary English*, *36* (Oct. 1959), 424-26.
29. Powell, Marvin, and Kenneth M. Parsley, Jr. "The Relationships Between First Grade Reading Readiness and Second Grade Reading Achievement," *Journal of Educational Research*, *54* (Feb. 1961), 229-33.

30. Rosen, Carl L. "A Study of Visual Perception Capabilities of First Grade Pupils and The Relationship Between Visual Perception Training and Reading Achievement," unpublished doctoral dissertation, University of Minnesota, 1965.
31. Rutherford, William L. "The Effect of a Perceptual-Motor Training Program on the Performance of Kindergarten Pupils on Metropolitan Readiness Tests," *Dissertation Abstracts, 25* (Feb. 1965), 4583-84.
32. Sheldon, William D., and Donald R. Lashinger. *Effect of First Grade Instruction Using Basal Readers, Modified Linguistic Materials and Linguistic Readers* (USOE Cooperative Research Project No. 2683). Syracuse, New York: Syracuse University, 1966.
33. Silberberg, Margaret C. "Effect of Formal Reading Readiness Training in Kindergarten," *Minnesota Reading Quarterly, 11* (Oct. 1966), 4-8.
34. Silvaroli, Nicholas Joseph. "Intellectual and Emotional Factors as Predictors of Children's Success in First Grade Reading," *Dissertation Abstracts, 24* (June 1964), 5098.
35. Spache, George D., Micaela C. Andres, H. A. Curtis, Minnie Lee Rowland, and Minnie Hall Fields. *A Study of a Longitudinal First Grade Reading Readiness Program* (USOE Cooperative Research Project No. 2742). Tallahassee, Florida: Florida State Department of Education, 1965.
36. Stauffer, Russell G., and W. Dorsey Hammond. *Effectiveness of a Language Arts and Basic Reader Approach to First Grade Reading Instruction* (USOE Cooperative Research Project No. 2679). Newark, Delaware: University of Delaware, 1965.
37. Tanyzer, Harold J., and Harvey Alpert. *Effectiveness of Three Different Basal Reading Systems on First Grade Reading Achievement* (USOE Cooperative Research Project No. 2720). Hempstead, New York: Hofstra University, 1965.
38. Thackray, D. V. "Summaries of Researches Reported in Degree Theses," *British Journal of Educational Psychology, 35* (June, 1965), 252-54.
39. Wright, W. W. *Reading Readiness: A Prognostic Study*, Bulletin of The School of Education, Indiana University, *12*, (June, 1936).

WILLIAM R. HARMER

UNIVERSITY OF TEXAS

5. The Selection and Use of Survey Reading Achievement Tests

STANDARDIZED survey reading achievement tests are used on an almost universal scale at the present time. Such tests are among the many administered in schools, reading laboratories, and reading clinics. Furthermore, they are available in a variety of sizes and shapes; *The Sixth Mental Measurements Yearbook* (3) lists 37 standardized survey reading achievement tests.

Since a wide variety of standardized survey reading achievement tests is so readily available, this paper is designed to focus attention on the intelligent selection and use of such instruments. To accomplish this task the remainder of the paper is divided into three parts. The first sets forth definitions of terms as they are used throughout the paper. The second establishes criteria which can be used in evaluating and selecting tests. Finally, some questions and recommendations regarding the use of results from survey reading achievement tests are discussed.

Definition of Terms

In the present context *standardized survey reading achievement tests* (Survey Reading Tests) are defined as tests which provide an average or general reading achievement score. Such tests will usually measure word recognition, gross comprehension, and in some cases rate of reading. There are some tests, however, that will assess five or more competencies on as many subtests or sections. In general, a survey reading test is not diagnostic or analytical in nature since its primary purpose is to provide an estimate of a pupil's overall reading ability.

Validity will usually be used in the generic sense here and it will refer to the question "Does the test measure what it purports to measure?" There will be occasions, however, when content or face validity will receive specific attention. In these instances, the reader will be made cognizant of this particular usage.

Reliability, as it is employed in this context, will refer to the consistency with which a test measures whatever it measures.

A fourth term that will be utilized throughout the paper is *agreement*. Agreement refers to the congruency of titles, tasks, and methods of measurement among various survey reading tests at a given grade level and across grade levels.

Finally, reference will be made to *norming group information*. In this instance, the use of this term will call attention to the types of children included in the sample upon which the norms were developed.

Criteria for Selecting Survey Reading Tests

Traxler and North (*15*) underscore the necessity for careful selection of tests in the following statement:

> The selection and administration of tests are among the more neglected aspects in the planning of a testing program because they often seem, at first thought, to be routine procedures that almost any teacher can handle with little or no preparation. On the contrary, wise choice of the specific tests to be used and careful administration of the tests to all pupils are critically important phases of a school testing program which call for a considerable amount of understanding and experience in educational measurement.

According to Townsend (*14*) in a recent review of reading tests in the *Sixth Mental Measurements Yearbook* (*3*), there is an increased sophistication of reviews of reading tests since the 1940's. This is reflected in the fact that reviewers tend to provide more rationale for both positive and negative reviews than had been true previously. While the trend is encouraging, it should be noted that Townsend's remarks dealt only with reviewers and not with consumers of tests. Is it possible, then, to infer that a corresponding increase of awareness of test strengths and weaknesses has occurred on the part of test users? Buros (*3*) states

> Although many test users undoubtedly are selecting and using tests with greater discrimination because of the *Mental Measurements Yearbooks*, there are many who are not. Despite unfavorable reviews in the *Mental Measurements Yearbooks*, the publication and use of inadequately validated tests seems to be keeping pace with the population explosion.

Assuming that Buros' analysis is accurate it seems appropriate to discuss some criteria which may be useful in selecting tests and to illustrate some of the problems a test consumer faces as he attempts to identify which test will best serve his purposes. The criteria are agreement, validity, reliability, and norming group information. Since information regarding agreement is not typically available in test manuals, as is the case with the other three criteria, it will be treated in much greater detail than validity, reliability, and norming group information.

Agreement Among Survey Reading Tests

As indicated previously, a wide variety of survey reading tests is available. Moreover, the task of determining agreement among such tests is complicated further by the multiplicity of terms and tasks used to designate and measure such abilities as word recognition, comprehension, and speed. For example, a review of the tests currently available reveals that there are subtests which carry such titles as accuracy, average comprehension, comprehension, specific comprehension, speed of comprehension, general comprehension, paragraph meaning, sentence and word meaning, vocabulary, word discrimination, word knowledge, and word recognition. This is by no means a complete list, but it serves to suggest a lack of agreement among test authors on the specific dimensions of reading which they are attempting to measure. McDonald (*11*) has discussed this problem at some length in a recent article.

Moreover, the divergency of titles raises at least two questions which affect the judgment of tests for any grade level. First, although titles may differ, are the tests for various grade levels in agreement in the tasks they require pupils to perform? Second, do tests which purport to measure the same or similar abilities measure them in the same way? These questions may be asked of tests at a given grade level or across grade levels. Following are some illustrations as they apply to tests for various grade levels. These illustrations may serve to clarify both the problem and the task of the test consumer.

Agreement among primary reading tests. At the primary grade level there seems to be a reasonable degree of uniformity in the dimensions of reading measured. Usually there are two, word recognition and comprehension. Beyond this point differences do appear to exist in terms of the names given to the dimensions and the way in which they are measured.

In the first instance, for example, word recognition is also called vocabulary, word knowledge, or word meaning by authors of tests. More important is the finding that this ability, whatever it is named, is measured in different ways. In some instances the testing task involves selecting from four choices a word which is associated with a picture, e.g., a rural scene with cows and a barn is presented and the child is to choose the word that labels the picture: *careful, along, bright,* or *country.*

Other tests measure this ability in different ways. Some include tasks which require the reading of brief, incomplete sentences or stems before selecting a word which converts the stem into a simple sentence. Some others require pupils to select from several printed choices an isolated word which has been pronounced by the teacher. It should be noted that this type of task requires the use of two sensory modalities. Auditory discrimination must be exercised in recognizing the word as the teacher pronounces it; visual discrimination must be exercised in identifying the printed symbol which represents the word. This is a somewhat different requirement than that of matching a word with a picture or selecting a word to complete a sentence, although all three tasks may carry similar labels.

With respect to the assessment of reading comprehension, most of the instruments prepared for use in the primary grades employ similar techniques. Again, there are some differences in the titles used from test to test, but the tasks across tests are essentially of three types. Some tests or subtests, with such titles as sentence meaning, reading comprehension, and following directions, require pupils to examine several pictures and mark them in accordance with directions given in sentence form. A slight variation of this task is provided by some other tests which present a single picture and require the selection of an appropriate sentence from among three or more which accompany the picture. A third type of comprehension test that appears is one where the child reads a short paragraph and demonstrates his understanding by recognizing what he read in a translated form.

In general, primary reading tests are more divergent in methods of measuring than in what they measure. It also appears that certain tests come closer to reflecting actual reading tasks than do others. Therefore, the people responsible for selecting reading tests for the primary grades should carefully consider test characteristics along with the validity, reliability, and norming group data on the tests before making any final decisions about purchasing a certain instrument.

Agreement among intermediate grade reading tests. An examination of the survey reading tests available for use at the intermediate grade level reveals that they possess some characteristics which are similar to those found in primary grade tests and some characteristics which set them apart from their primary grade counterparts. With respect to the similarities, the intermediate grade tests do purport to measure word knowledge and comprehension in most cases as did the primary grade tests. There is also a continuation in the lack of agreement among test authors in labeling the subtests used to measure these two reading abilities. Moreover, as was the case when primary grade tests were studied, the tasks used to measure what appears to be the same ability may be quite different from test to test.

The differences between the primary and intermediate survey reading tests appear to be four in number. First, intermediate grade tests rarely use pictures. As a result, the pupil cannot rely on picture clues for help. Second, the test titles allude to the measurement of more specific comprehension abilities than those found in the primary grades, e.g., main ideas, following directions, facts, etc. Third, there is some emphasis given to reading rate and accuracy at this level, while no such emphasis was noted in the primary grade tests. Finally, it appears that there is a greater effort on the part of the authors of the intermediate grade tests to go beyond the literal meaning level in general comprehension tasks by requiring inferences on the part of the reader. Although more of this latter task might be in order, it appears that some effort has been made in this direction at the intermediate grade level.

Agreement among secondary and college reading tests. In general, the comments made about the characteristics of the survey reading tests designed for use at the lower grade levels are applicable to the tests designed for use at the higher levels. Without belaboring the point, the most salient features of the advanced level tests are their concern for measuring different types or levels of comprehension and the divergency in the ways they attempt to accomplish this task, even when the same type of comprehension ability is in question. With regard to the need to consider these characteristics carefully when selecting tests at this level, the works of Bligh (*2*), Cleland (*5*), McDonald (*10*), and Vogel (*16*), are worth noting. For example, Bligh, Cleland, and McDonald have called attention to the differences in tasks which purport to measure similar abilities. Some of the differences they pointed out were (a) a single, abbreviated paragraph versus a long selection; (b) literal comprehension versus a thorough interpretation; and (c) time limits which do include the time used to answer items versus time limits which do not include the time used to answer items.

A study reported by Emans, Urbas, and Dummett (*6*) also dealt with the intrinsic differences of tests which purport to perform the same measurement task. For example, the authors examined two tests. One test was written at the third grade level, consisted of short paragraphs, and required responses to questions during the timed period. The second test was written at the high school level, consisted of lengthy selections, and required responses after a timed reading period. On the basis of the descriptions of the two tests, the investigators concluded that although both tests measured the same ability, the methods of measurement were different. Certainly, both tests were apparently measuring reading comprehension, but the ability was being measured in two very different fashions.

Selecting Survey Reading Tests in Perspective

The diverse nature of survey reading tests at all levels indicates that those who are responsible for selecting such tests must consider many factors before making their final decisions. One of the major concerns of test selectors should be the agreement among tests with respect to what subtest titles indicate is being measured and the methods used to measure the ability indicated by the title. Beyond this consideration, however, test selectors should also delve into the matter of the demonstrated reliability and validity of a test and the nature of the group upon which the norms were based. The need for this type of information when tests are being considered for selection was underscored by Traxler and North (*15*):

> The selection and administration of tests are among the more neglected aspects in the planning of a testing program because they often seem, at first thought, to be routine procedures that almost any teacher can handle with little or no preparation. On the contrary, wise choice of the specific tests to be used and careful administration of the tests to all pupils are critically important phases of a school testing program which call for a considerable amount of understanding and experience in educational measurement.

The Use of Survey Reading Tests

It would appear to be as important in the last half of the 1960's, as it was throughout the 1940's and 1950's, to urge all individuals who purchase and use reading tests not only to investigate the validity and reliability of these instruments, but also to consider their appropriateness. An illustration of inappropriate use of a survey reading test may add needed emphasis to this point. In the southwestern states, a sizable number of first grade pupils of Mexican-American parentage come from homes where Spanish is the dominant or only language spoken. The schools which these children attend, however, are conducted in English and, in some instances, speaking Spanish in school is forbidden by law. It does not seem reasonable to expect a reading test, administered in English, to assess adequately a bilingual child's level of reading instruction let alone yield an estimate of his capacity for learning to read. Yet this practice, although somewhat reduced in recent years, continues to exist in a number of school systems. The test, a widely used and well-rated battery, is not at fault. It simply was never intended for use with non-English speaking youngsters. The misuse of this test with these children is, or should be, of more than academic concern to educators. The combination of mis-selection, misuse, and misinterpretation of reading tests has often spelled out individual tragedy, while perpetuating a cycle of low academic expectation and a resultingly poor performance from children of a minority group.

How can such misuses of survey reading tests be avoided? Test consumers must keep this question in mind constantly. It also seems that test consumers must keep a second question in the forefront of their thoughts: "What is the purpose for testing?" In general, the response to the latter question is that the basic purpose is to assist the teacher in determining a pupil's reading proficiency in order to provide appropriate instruction. Whether the information acquired from the test is used in grouping youngsters for instruction, for providing individual instruction, or for detecting youngsters who require additional study and testing, it must be related in some way to instruction. Testing for the sake of testing cannot be countenanced. Test results that are not used as instructional aids constitute unnecessary expense, effort, and wasted time, all of which are ill-afforded by our schools.

The remainder of this section of the paper, then, discusses four factors related to the uses of standardized survey reading achievement tests: (a) grade scores as indicators of functional reading levels; (b) the comparability of test results from one test to another; (c) the use of alternate forms of the same test; and (d) the use of tests designed for a narrow range of students as opposed to those designed for a broader range of students.

Grade Scores on Standardized Tests as Indicators of Functional Reading Levels

Should grade scores on standardized tests be considered as indicators of a pupil's frustration reading level, his instructional reading level, or his independent reading level? This question was considered by three investigators who used reading levels achieved on informal reading inventories as the criteria for determining functional reading levels.

In the first instance, Sipay (*13*) compared the results of three well-known standardized reading tests with the achievement levels on an informal reading inventory. He found that, even when the word pronunciation accuracy criterion was lowered from 95 to 90 percent on the informal inventory, two of the three standardized tests yielded significantly higher grade placement scores than did the informal inventory.

In an earlier study which also employed an informal reading inventory and standardized reading tests, Harbiger (*8*) found that the difference between the subjects' achievement levels on standardized reading tests and informal reading inventory was substantial. This finding led him to conclude that the results of standardized tests more often than not place children at their frustration reading levels.

It is important to note that both the Sipay and Harbiger studies were carried out in normal classroom situations. Thus, the children in their samples are presumed to have been representative of the average range of achievement.

Arnold and Arnold (*1*), on the other hand, conducted a study of measured reading levels of severely disabled readers at a university psycho-educational clinic. The results of the investigations were based on comparisons of reading achievement determined by standardized reading tests, an informal reading inventory, and judgments by reading clinicians and tutors. Not too surprising was the finding that the standardized tests rated pupils at a higher level than did clinicians and tutors. However, when the results reported by Sipay and Harbiger were used as a point of reference, the Arnold and Arnold finding that the informal inventory rated the subjects higher than the standardized tests was somewhat unexpected.

What, then, do these three studies mean when they are considered together? A conclusion which might be drawn from the Sipay and Harbiger studies is that standardized reading tests tend to overrate pupils when compared to informal inventories. However, the conflict between the results of the Arnold and Arnold study and the Sipay and Harbiger studies underscores the necessity for noting differences in pupil achievement characteristics before employing any generalization pertinent to the relative merits of standardized and informal reading scores as indicators of functional reading levels.

Sipay (*13*) probably summed up the situation best with this statement:

> ... It is impossible to generalize whether standardized reading achievement scores indicate the instructional or frustration level. Rather, it appears in making such judgments, one must consider the standardized reading test used and the criteria employed to estimate functional reading levels.

Of course, one might take the position that if the tests used are valid, reliable, and based on norm groups which bear some resemblance to the children being tested, more faith can be placed in their ability to place children at their functional reading levels. The presence of these factors does not, however, resolve the problem of possible differences between test scores and functional reading levels. The dangers of accepting reading test results as absolute have been repeatedly pointed out by scholars in the field (*5, 4, 13, 10*). The following constitutes a summary of cautions to be exercised in this context:

  a. Test users should keep in mind that the test score is simply the result of performance on a particular day, at a particular time, and in a particular testing environment.
  b. The diagnosis of reading achievement through the use of standardized tests may be fallacious unless carelessness and attitudes toward taking tests on the part of students are controlled.
  c. The grade score on a standardized reading achievement test should not be thought of as precise indication of overall reading achievement; rather, it should be thought of as a measure of reading ability on that test at a particular point in time.

d. Teachers should keep in mind that the grade scores on standardized tests are derived by interpolating scores between grade levels or by extrapolating scores from one grade level to another; thus, grade scores cannot be treated as empirically obtained indications of month-to-month progress.

The point of the preceding cautions is that teachers may well be deceived if they interpret a grade score from a survey reading test as a precise estimate of a functional reading level, either instructional or independent. Moreover, if the deception is in the direction of overestimating reading ability and is transferred to the pupils by having them use reading materials that are too difficult, the result may very well reduce the possibility of success and may in turn develop negative attitudes toward reading on the part of the students. Contrarily, if the deception is in the direction of underestimating reading ability, boredom may result which could also develop into negative attitudes toward reading on the part of the pupils. In general, then, it appears that the grade scores on standardized tests should be used only as a point of departure for determining functional reading levels.

Comparability of Scores From Different Tests

Another problem associated with the use of survey reading tests involves the comparability of scores from different tests. An earlier reference was made to conflicting results obtained from different tests when they were administered to the same pupils. Even if the results were not conflicting, the question as to whether or not they indicated the same kind of proficiency remains unresolved. To illustrate this point further, consider a study reported by Fortenberry and Broome (7). In it they compared the results of two standardized reading tests—one a test of speed, vocabulary, and comprehension, and the other a test of word pronunciation skills. Correlation coefficients between each of the subtests on the first test and the word pronunciation were .67, .68, and .80. When appropriate statistical tests were applied to the correlation coefficients, all were found to be significantly different from zero at or beyond the .01 level. Do these findings justify an assumption that when test results are the same, or quite similar, they have the same meaning? A negative response to this question was expressed by Bligh (2).

> The problem of comparability of test scores continued to be an enigma to test developers and test users. Two aspects of the problem were generally recognized: (a) the nonequivalence of norm groups and (b) the marked content differences of tests intended to measure the same traits.

In general, it is recommended that reading test results be viewed in terms of their source. Certainly, the illustrations and opinions presented suggest that to accept a reading grade score at face value may be as deceptive as buying a pair of shoes without trying them on.

Using Alternate Forms of the Same Test

Another facet of the problem of comparability of test scores is the use of alternate forms of the same test. While most of the more commonly used tests of reading are available in two, three, or four alternate forms, an assumption that the tests are the same may not necessarily be warranted. A not infrequent request for more evidence concerning the relative difficulty or equivalence of alternate forms of the same test is expressed in reviews of reading tests in *The Sixth Mental Measurements Yearbook* (3). The requests do not indicate a general rejection of the alternate forms, but, rather, raise questions regarding comparability of difficulty, of content, and of grade scores. In some instances, the technical manuals which accompany the tests do indeed furnish evidence of the equivalency of forms. There are, however, some tests which furnish little or no evidence to substantiate the comparability of their alternate forms.

An additional question in regard to the comparability of alternate forms is raised by Karlin and Jolly (9). Their study, which involved the administration of two reading tests at the beginning of the school year and the administration of the same tests plus alternate forms at the end of the year, indicated that no real justification existed for the use of alternate forms. The results of the study indicated that contamination from the use of the same test form at the beginning and end of the school year was negligible. While it might be rash to embrace these findings for an immediate, general application, it would be less than scientific not to give them consideration and seek additional information.

Grade Span and the Use of Tests

The point to be considered here is whether a test of broad grade span— one designed for use in grades three through ten—is as effective throughout its range as a test of more limited grade span, one designed for use in grades four through six. Without taking issue with the difference in reading task requirements, it may be stated with reasonable certainty that broad range tests tend to produce more mis-measurements at their extremes than do tests of the same type which are more restricted in range. Therefore, while a broad range test may be quite suitable for use in the grades which are in the middle of its range, it may be inappropriately easy or difficult for those grades at or near the upper and lower ends of its grade span. Users of these tests would do well to regard extremely high or low scores with some skepticism, particularly when they are earned by pupils in those grades at either end of the tests' grade span.

Conclusion

It seems appropriate to pose a number of questions which teachers and other test users might ask in regard to the selection and use of survey reading tests.
1. *Why is a test to be given?*
   If the response to this question is centered more around determining a pupil's past progress than on determining his present status, a reexamination of the relation of a testing program to instruction is necessary
2. *How will the test results be used?*
   Unless a specific instructional answer is made to this question, the administration, scoring, and recording of the results may have become a meaningless exercise in conformity.
3. *Is the test appropriate for the pupils?*
   This is a rather broad question and its facets include chronological age, intelligence, culture, and previous instruction. One basic question to be answered is: "Did the standardization of the test include groups whose characteristics are the same as those of the pupils with whom the test will be used?"
4. *Does the test assess those pupil competencies which are the teaching objectives?*
   If the testing is not directly related to what is being taught, what purpose does it serve? If, for example, comprehension is being stressed in instruction, a test of word pronunciation skills may be of some value but will not provide an adequate assessment.
5. *Is the test valid and reliable?*
   Does the test measure what it is supposed to measure and can it be depended upon to be consistent in that measurement? Such information may normally be found in technical manuals which often are available from the publishers. In addition, it is strongly recommended that a current edition of the *Mental Measurements Yearbook* (*3*) be consulted for additional evaluations.

Other questions, such as those dealing with the breadth of grade span and the relationship of test results to functional levels, should be given consideration as facets of questions three, four, and five.

If survey reading tests are to be used at all, they should be chosen thoughtfully, used cautiously in accordance with their stated requirements and procedures, and interpreted carefully. Reading tests should be the servants, not the dictators, of reading instruction.

REFERENCES

1. Arnold, Bettie B., and Richard D. Arnold. "The Assessment of Reading Level for Disabled Readers," *Elementary School Journal*, (in press).
2. Bligh, Harold F. "Trends in the Measurement of Educational Achievement," *Review of Educational Research, 35* (February 1965), 34-52.
3. Buros, Oscar K. *The Sixth Mental Measurements Yearbook*. Highland Park, New Jersey: The Gryphon Press, 1965.
4. Chansky, Norman M. "A Note on the Validity of Reading Test Scores," *Journal of Educational Research, 48* (October 1964), 30.
5. Cleland, Donald L. "Clinical Materials for Appraising Disabilities in Reading," *The Reading Teacher, 17* (March 1964), 428-34.
6. Emans, Robert, Raymond Urbas, and Marjorie Dummett. "The Meaning of Reading Tests," *Journal of Reading, 9* (May 1966), 406-7.
7. Fortenberry, Warren D., and Billy J. Broome. "Comparison of the Gates Reading Survey and the Reading Section of the Wide Range Achievement Test," *Journal of Developmental Reading, 7* (Autumn 1963), 66-68.
8. Harbiger, Sister Mary Joan, O.S.F. "Comparative Study of the Level of Reading Established by Standardized Tests and Actual Reading Levels Determined by Informal Tests," *Research Abstracts*, The Cardinal Stritch College, Milwaukee, Wisconsin, *1* (1958-59), 8-12.
9. Karlin, Robert, and Hayden Jolly. "The Use of Alternate Forms of Standardized Reading Tests," *The Reading Teacher, 19* (December 1965), 187-91.
10. McDonald, Arthur S. "Some Pitfalls in Evaluating Progress in Reading Instruction," *Phi Delta Kappan, 45* (April 1964), 336-38.
11. McDonald, Arthur S. "Using Standardized Tests to Determine Reading Proficiency," *Journal of Reading, 8* (October 1964), 58-61.
12. Robinson, H. Alan. "Critique of Current Research in College and Adult Reading," in Eric L. Thurston and Lawrence E. Hafner, (Eds.), *New Concepts in College-Adult Reading: Thirteenth Yearbook of the National Reading Conference*. Milwaukee, Wisconsin: National Reading Conference, Inc., 1964.
13. Sipay, Edward R. "A Comparison of Standardized Reading Scores and Functional Reading Levels," *The Reading Teacher, 17* (January 1964), 265-68.
14. Townsend, Agatha. "Search and Research in Testing," *The Reading Teacher, 19* (February 1966), 371-79.
15. Traxler, Arthur E., and Robert D. North. "The Selection and Use of Tests in a School Testing Program," *The Impact and Improvement of School Testing Programs: The Sixty-Second Yearbook of the National Society for the Study of Education, Part II*. Chicago: University of Chicago Press, 1963.
16. Vogel, Alfred T. "An Examination of Reading Tests," *High Points, 46* (June 1964), 12-18.

WALLACE RAMSEY

UNIVERSITY OF KENTUCKY

6. The Values and Limitations of Diagnostic Reading Tests for Evaluation in the Classroom

THE classroom teacher who seeks ways to evaluate the reading potential and ability of the children under her care will find an almost bewildering array of published tests and other instruments to assist her. In fact, the number available and the variety of abilities appraised by them make a wise selection very difficult.

Each of the available instruments has its shortcomings, so much so that it is the writer's impression that very few reading clinics use one, or even a few, of these in their diagnosis. On the contrary, the informal reading inventory and various other teacher-made and clinician-made instruments seem to be very popular in the centers whose main activity is the careful diagnosis of reading problems.

Nevertheless, the classroom teacher who lacks the training or the time to construct or administer informal instruments will find certain standardized measures of substantial value in helping her gain insight into the reading strengths, weaknesses, and potential of her pupils. The greatest advantage in using such instruments lies in the fact that they have been, for the most part, constructed by persons of substantial training, experience, and reputation. Such people as Donald Durrell, Marian Monroe, Arthur Gates, George Spache, Guy Bond, Morton Botel, and their colleagues have great insights into the nature of reading and the ways that reading disabilities manifest themselves. Their experiences in clinical reading qualify them to construct instruments designed to be most revealing about areas of concern.

The writer is not well acquainted with all of the diagnostic reading tests currently available. This prevents a complete and exhaustive discussion. The following are the most widely used tests of this nature and the discussion in this paper will be largely restricted to them:

1. Botel Reading Inventory
2. California Phonics Survey

3. Developmental Reading Tests: Silent Reading, Diagnostic Tests
4. Diagnostic Reading Tests
5. Durrell Analysis of Reading Difficulty
6. Gates-McKillop Reading Diagnostic Tests
7. Gilmore Oral Reading Test
8. Gray Oral Reading Test
9. McCullough Word-Analysis Tests
10. McKee Inventory of Phonetic Skills
11. Monroe Diagnostic Reading Examination
12. Spache Diagnostic Reading Scales

Trella has recently described six of the foregoing tests in terms of the skills they analyze (*16*). More comprehensive discussions have been made by Bond and Tinker (*12*), Harris (*13*), and Zintz (*17*).

General Values of Diagnostic Tests

The diagnostic reading tests discussed in this paper have numerous general values for the classroom teacher. Several of the tests provide a series of unfamiliar but carefully graded paragraphs for oral and silent reading testing. The paragraphs usually have been especially prepared for the test (and are therefore likely to be unfamiliar to the child) and the levels of difficulty have been carefully determined. The use of the paragraphs, following the procedures prescribed in the test manual, or following the teacher's own procedures which she may use because her expectations concerning reading performance are different from those of the test maker, is likely to reveal much valuable knowledge about the child's reading. For reasons to be noted later in this paper, this may be their most valued advantage.

In addition, some of the tests provide graded lists of words to use in determining the size and level of a poor reader's sight vocabulary and his word analysis ability. The words on such lists are usually very carefully chosen and grade level established according to discrete and important criteria.

Some of the tests include special sections designed to reveal information about reversals, word blending, and other specific word analysis skills. Some items of this type are ingeniously devised and their construction calls for more creativity than many teachers have.

Most of the tests have norms for many of their subtests so that it is possible to determine how a given student's performance compares with that of other students of various ages and grade levels. Such information is highly useful in communicating test results to other teachers, to parents, and occasionally to the child himself.

An ultimate value of several of the tests is that they present a model for systematic analysis of reading skills, a model devised by an authority in reading, a model likely to be more nearly all-inclusive of the skills needing testing than a procedure derived by the average classroom teacher. The use of or even acquaintance with the test will stimulate the teacher to make a more comprehensive analysis of reading abilities than she might otherwise make. For this reason, if for no other, such tests are worth buying and studying very carefully.

In the diagnosis of reading there is a need for instruments to evaluate *many* abilities in reading. A battery of minimum value will include measures of oral reading, silent reading, and word perception skills, including sight vocabulary and phonics. A measure of reading potential, either an individual intelligence test administered by a trained person or a listening test that has been skillfully constructed, well standardized, and carefully administered, is highly desirable. Tests of such word perception skills as use of context, reversals, and structural analysis are certainly useful. There is no one diagnostic test that will do all these things. There are some that do *most* of them, and it is always possible to put together a collection of tests to do the job.

Desirable Criteria for Diagnostic Tests

There are several criteria that should be met by diagnostic reading tests. Some of these that are especially important are listed and explained below. Each has been given a label which will be used in referring to it in discussing specific diagnostic tests in remaining sections of this paper.

The *reality* criterion is of primary importance. If a test meets this criterion it will test an ability in much the same manner as the ability is used in real reading. If it is not met, then an accurate appraisal of a specific ability by the test in question is not possible and conclusions drawn concerning student responses may not be valid. Examples of conformity or the lack of conformity to this criterion will be given later. It should be noted that it is not always possible for all items in a test to meet this criterion completely while meeting all those listed below.

The *guessing* criterion is met when it is *not* possible for the student to *guess* the correct answer to an item. The purpose of diagnosis is to make possible corrective teaching that is specific to the student's needs. Therefore, the examiner should not be forced to entertain the possibility that the student can guess the correct answer to an item. The possibility of guessing can never be eliminated but the nature of the desired response to an item can reduce the possibility of guessing. Poor readers will quite often guess wildly on multiple-choice tests. They have usually had trouble with tests and have learned that they have little to lose by guessing. They frequently inflate their test scores by such behavior.

The *active* criterion is met if the desired response demands some overt, observable behavior from the student as he reacts to an item. This is necessary so that the examiner can clearly discern the nature of the student's response. Tests of ability in phonics especially need to meet this criterion as well as the *specificity* criterion. The latter criterion is met if an item measures a specific ability rather than a constellation of abilities.

The *comprehension* criterion is especially important in tests of oral and silent reading. The criterion is met if items checking the understanding of what is read actually test *comprehension* and *interpretation* rather than pure *memory* of what has been read. Some poor readers can remember very well what they read but understand little of it. A student whose teachers have stressed remembering rather than understanding will tend to read to attain that objective. It would be foolish to contend that memory is not involved in understanding but understanding involves many more—and more important—abilities. Thorndike's study (*15*) of reading as reasoning established this principle almost fifty years ago.

No one test could completely meet all of the above criteria, due to differences in the abilities to be tested and the kinds of responses that are possible. In some cases one criterion may be intrinsically at odds with another. In such cases arbitrary decisions are necessary concerning which criterion shall be met.

Complete Diagnostic Batteries

There are four batteries of diagnostic reading tests that contain material and directions for comprehension evaluation of reading abilities. These are the Durrell, Gates, Monroe, and Spache Diagnostic Tests. All must be given to one child at a time.

The Durrell, Gates, and Monroe tests constitute three of the oldest complete batteries of diagnostic reading tests. Each of the three, with its component parts, tends to give a complete picture of a child's strengths and weaknesses. The Durrell evaluates both oral and silent reading, a desirable attribute. The Monroe and Gates evaluate oral reading only. Recent revisions of the first two tend to make them more up-to-date than the Monroe. The Monroe does not evaluate as many abilities as the Gates or Durrell and its lack of recent revision makes it less popular.

The Gates test provides a set of reading paragraphs which increase in difficulty and tell a continuous story, but there is only one paragraph at each level in the test booklet and there are no comprehension questions. This condition plus the lack of a test of silent reading greatly reduces the effectiveness of the battery. However, the battery is probably more suitable than the Durrell test for diagnosing the problems of the severely retarded reader.

The Durrell provides tests of both oral and silent reading, but neither the oral nor the silent reading paragraphs tell a continuous story. The comprehension questions in the oral section are almost exclusively of the memory type—there is almost a complete absence of questions evaluating the ability to draw inferences, get the main idea, note the sequence of ideas, or draw conclusions from what is read. There are no questions over the silent reading (except some *optional* ones referring to imagery), but the student is asked to tell what he *remembers* of the selection. Credit in comprehension depends upon the number of ideas remembered and repeated.

The oral reading tests of the Gates, Durrell, and Monroe, as well as all of the oral reading tests described in this paper, can be very revealing if a careful recording and analysis is made of pupils' oral reading errors on the tests. Several systems for manual recording of pupil errors have been devised. All of them provide for crossing out, underlining, and writing in by the examiner on a copy of the material being read.

Classroom teachers who have not had much practice in doing this are likely to find that their marking cannot keep pace with the student's reading. Such marking is distracting to the student and may tend to influence his performance negatively. Therefore, it is recommended that the student's oral reading of the test material be tape recorded. This can be made less distracting than written recording and is likely to render the errors more amenable to careful analysis.

Oral reading is suitable for noting word recognition errors and not much else of major importance. It is true that phrasing ability and attention to punctuation can be noted. These in themselves are unimportant, unless one uses oral reading much more extensively, or for more important purposes than the usual person does—except as indicators of obtained meaning. Because the oral reading task is so complex, the presence or absence of attention to phrasing and punctuation do not necessarily indicate whether or not the meaning is being understood.

In many schools there is an overemphasis on oral reading and sounding out of words. Students get the impression that this is all there is to reading and are concerned with nothing else. Many fluent oral readers have trouble in understanding what they read.

There is some evidence that the oral and silent reading selections in most standardized reading diagnostic tests are too short for perceptually handicapped children. Shedd (*14*) has indicated that the children with specific perceptual motor disabilities with whom he has worked in the Berea (Kentucky) project do not mobilize as rapidly as normal children and therefore make many more mistakes in the first paragraph they read than they do in later paragraphs. Given the great degree of distractibility of such children and their tendency to inattention and hyperactive motor discharge, effective diagnostic testing of them is extremely tedious and difficult and not possible for most classroom teachers.

Silent reading performance is much more valid for testing comprehension than is oral reading. Careful questioning after silent reading, which utilizes many types of questions (main idea, detail, inference, sequence, background, vocabulary, etc.), is the best way of assessing understanding. Most, if not all, of the standardized reading diagnostic tests do not provide for this kind of questioning. Most are tests of memory for what is read, in itself of importance but not of exclusive importance.

Both the Gates and the Durrell provide tests of sight vocabulary using a hand tachistoscope. The use of such a device provides a highly artificial way of testing such vocabulary and may distract some children to such a degree that it keeps them from giving a true indication of what they know. Nevertheless, it seems to be a *fair* way of evaluating sight vocabulary if it is preceded by a short session orienting and accustoming the child to the device. The Durrell method of tachistoscopic testing is much more convenient than the Gates, and the word list used is more extensive and more carefully graded.

On both tests children are given unflashed (untimed) tests of word analysis. On the Durrell a child is asked to analyze a word only if he cannot recognize it when flashed. This seems to be a better procedure than that used in the Gates, a test in which a child might recognize as sight words most of the words to be "analyzed."

The Gates tests the child's recognition of phrases; the Durrell does not. Both test the ability to name letters. Both have tests which ask the child to indicate which letter spells the first sound of a word, or which word begins like a word pronounced by the examiner. Both fail to meet the criterion of *guessing* and are subject to the same defect as that found in the McKee Phonics Tests, namely, that testing the ability to identify the way a spoken sound is spelled is not testing the same ability as that called for in supplying the sound of a letter appearing in writing. The Gates Nonsense Word Test is subject to the same limitation. The auditory blending part of the test is valid only if used with children who have been taught phonics by a synthetic (sound blending) method. The same can be said of the Durrell Sounds of Letters test.

The Durrell test, Learning to Hear Sounds in Words, is a very useful one, as is the Test of Listening Comprehension, except that the latter utilizes questions that are largely of the memory type. The tests of spelling (Gates and Durrell), and Durrell's handwriting test are only of general interest and value in a reading analysis.

Spache's Diagnostic Reading Scales is a fairly comprehensive battery of diagnostic reading tests of recent origin. It is designed for individual administration, contains tests of both oral and silent reading, and has six short supplementary phonics tests. A multi-level word recognition test of 130 words, spanning grade levels one through six, can be used to test sight vocabulary and establish a starting level for the oral and silent reading. A series of 22 reading passages at various grade levels from primer to eighth grade can be used for oral and silent reading testing. These range in length from thirty words at early first grade level to over two hundred at eighth grade level. Comprehension questions, with seven or eight questions per passage, are given for checking understanding. The questions do not meet the *comprehension* criterion since they are chiefly of the variety that test *memory* for what is read, rather than testing understanding. The paragraphs themselves seem to be carefully written and the difficulty carefully established.

Norming of the test appears adequate, although establishing validity by showing high correlation with one specific reading survey test seems questionable. The survey test used sets individual reading levels significantly higher than other similar tests of high repute. Directions are given for establishing "reading potential level" using the 22 paragraphs. This is done by determining the highest level at which the pupil understands the paragraphs when they are read to him. The lack of questions evaluating the various *kinds* of comprehension reduces the usefulness of this part of the test.

The phonics tests do not meet the *reality* criterion and call for responses that would be normal only for a child taught phonics by synthetic methods.

Despite the limitations noted, all of the tests described above, especially the Spache and Durrell, are highly useful tests. They have been carefully constructed, are fairly comprehensive, and will prove very valuable to one who administers them carefully. They are time consuming, but their results are worth the time.

Botel Reading Inventory

The Botel is discussed apart from the others, because it is partly a group test and samples fewer abilities than those previously treated. It consists of four parts: (a) tests of word recognition on grade levels 1-4, (b-c) word opposites, a test of reading and listening comprehension, and (d) a phonics mastery test. The word opposites and phonics mastery tests may be given as group tests; the test of word recognition is an individual test. It is designed chiefly for pupils reading at levels up to fourth grade.

Colleagues at the University of Illinois, Saint Cloud (Minnesota) State College, and the University of Massachusetts have reported that they teach the use of this inventory in their classes for preservice and in-service teachers. We have used it in the Reading Center at the University of Kentucky and have found it to be a useful instrument for teacher education in reading. We have been disappointed in its value for use with children. The results obtained have not been discrete enough for individualized remedial reading work. It cannot be said to what extent the inventory would detect group weaknesses.

The value of the use of Word Opposites Test as a test of listening comprehension is based on the idea that a pupil's listening ability is a direct indication of his reading *potential*. The writer has no quarrel with this idea, but the Botel test seems to be only an incomplete test of listening vocabulary. It does not meet the *guessing* criterion. Even if it did, a much more comprehensive test of listening ability would be needed.

The phonics mastery test is by far the most useful and valid test in the battery. It tests the major phonic abilities by determining the child's ability to *spell* certain sound combinations. By testing the abilities in this way it fails to meet the *reality* criterion, since the ability to spell certain sound patterns is not the same as the ability to supply sound equivalents for patterns of print. Nevertheless, it is superior to most phonics mastery tests.

The Test of Word Recognition appears to be a valid test of sight words *in isolation* (as they seldom appear in real reading). However, it should be pointed out that they are tested in an untimed situation where they may be analyzed, if the child wishes. Since the words are taken from a standardized grade list, the child may or may not have had a chance to learn them as sight words. This test seems to fail to meet the criterion of *reality*.

The Word Opposites Test used as a test of reading comprehension is an unusual test. It purports to test comprehension by measuring the pupil's ability to select a word that is the opposite of another word. It is, to the writer, more of a test of reading vocabulary and not a particularly valid test at that. A child might do poorly on it because he did not recognize the words; another child might do well on it and still have difficulty in comprehending phrases, sentences, and paragraphs.

Oral Reading Tests

The Gray Oral Reading Test is a recent revision—actually a rewriting—of the traditionally useful Gray Oral Reading Paragraphs and Check Tests. It consists of thirteen reading selections that range in length from twenty to fifty words, and vary in levels of difficulty from preprimer to adult level. For each selection there are four questions which can be correctly answered by oral reproduction of the words of the text or by paraphrasing it. The questions do not meet the *comprehension* criterion. The selections appear to be carefully graded—all are of a narrative variety but do not tell a continuous story. In scoring the test the word recognition errors must be recorded, and the time taken to read each selection must be carefully noted. There are four different forms of the test. The test is very valuable for noting weaknesses in word perception. The norms seem quite high—the test tends to underestimate children's instructional reading levels. The reading selections are too short for establishing instructional level in a dependable way.

The Gilmore Test consists of a series of ten paragraphs that range in length from 26 to 250 words and in difficulty from preprimer to grade eight and tell a continuous story. The five comprehension questions that accompany each story ask chiefly for direct recall of the material. The selections are interesting and seem to be well graded. Their greater length makes them more useful than the Gray paragraphs.

Either the Gray or the Gilmore are satisfactory for use in determining word perception strengths and abilities—insofar as this can be done through oral reading. Neither has a test of the specific abilities of phonics. Since both are only oral reading tests their usefulness is limited.

Higher Level Diagnostic Tests

The battery named The Diagnostic Reading Tests, published by the Committee on Diagnostic Reading Tests, is one of the few batteries designed for use with average readers in high school. The Committee also publishes similar batteries for use with children in grades one through eight. The diagnostic battery consists of seven separate tests: one each of vocabulary and comprehension, tests of oral and silent word attack, and three tests of rate. All are designed for group administration. Each test takes from twenty minutes to an hour to administer.

The test would have many different uses for teachers of reading or content subjects to determine general *class* strengths or weaknesses. Several criteria for diagnostic tests are not met. The student can have a field day guessing on the tests. The tests do not meet the *specificity* criterion. In many cases an error on a particular item might mean any one of several things.

The vocabulary tests have too small a sample of vocabulary from any one field—athough not as small as some of the more widely-used survey tests. They violate the *specificity* criterion since a person may miss items because he cannot pronounce the words on the test rather than because he does not know word meanings.

The writer has the highest regard for the comprehension section of the test. It requires the student to read material from several different subject fields and answer multiple-choice questions of several different types. By analyzing the student's responses some impression of his ability to comprehend material in different subject fields may be obtained; there are no directions to assist the examiner in doing this. A good test of *listening comprehension* (therefore, of reading potential) of subject matter in different content fields can be given by using one of four forms of the comprehension test, reading it to students and having them answer the comprehension questions.

The rate tests have in the past been withdrawn from sale for revision or restandardization. They would be useful to determine pupils' rates of reading in general reading material, social studies material, or science material.

The word attack (silent) test is more a test of auditory discrimination than of word attack. It is doubtful if an analysis of errors on it would help a teacher determine what word attack weaknesses a student had. The word attack (oral) will fill the same role as the Gray Oral or the Gilmore except that it contains selections of higher difficulty—up to and including grade twelve.

The tests seem to be expensive but the possibility of reuse reduces the per student cost. However, the test booklets are not very sturdy and do not seem durable.

The tests are misnamed: they are not diagnostic tests in the strictest sense but are actually survey tests that do a more extensive job than the usual survey test—and are therefore possibly more reliable than most survey tests.

Tests of Word Attack

The California Phonics Survey, the Bond-Clymer, the McCullough Tests, and the McKee Tests are all instruments designed to evaluate word attack abilities.

As the title indicates, the California is designed for use as a *survey* test from grade level seven through college and is included here because of its uniqueness. It is intended for group administration: all items have multiple-choice answers. The student *listens* and marks his booklet to indicate if a pronounced sound cluster is spelled out, or if a pronounced word is spelled out in his test booklet, etc. By testing phonics abilities in this way it violates the criterion of *reality*. Using the given directions, errors on the California may be readily analyzed to determine the student's weaknesses in various areas of phonics. It is doubtful that remedial teaching could be adequately planned, even after an analysis of test results, without more information concerning students' abilities in phonics.

The Bond-Clymer is a group test utilizing the multiple-choice format. According to the manual, it is designed for children reading at third grade level and above, but it would not be useful with readers above grade level eight. The California might be more appropriate above that level.

The Bond-Clymer purports to test twelve different word attack abilities in the areas of sight recognition, phonics, use of context, and structural analysis—syllabification and root words. The test seems to be carefully constructed and fairly comprehensive. All sections violate the *guessing* criterion because of the multiple-choice format. Some areas violate the *reality* criterion—including the "Locating Elements," e.g., the word *entirely* is printed under the picture of a tire; the student is expected to "find that little word in the big word below the picture." "Word Synthesis" is when words are broken at unnatural places at the end of a line of print, e.g., *stick* is broken ST-ICK with the second part located below and to the left of the first. The tests of the use of context and reversals are unique and useful portions of the battery. The test might be useful in some *corrective* reading classes; however, the writer has found that the level of teacher knowledge in corrective reading techniques must be exceptionally high if he is to make practical use of Bond-Clymer test results.

The McCullough Word-Analysis Tests contain seven subtests, five concerning phonics abilities and two measuring structural analysis abilities. The phonics subtests utilize the multiple-choice format and therefore violate the *guessing* criterion; two of these ask the child to *listen* and choose letters that spell the initial consonant or medial vowel sound. These violate the *reality* criterion. One subtest is a sound-matching exercise (letter combinations spelling the same sound combinations are matched)—a test of auditory discrimination, one important ability in learning phonics.

A fourth phonics subtest asks the student to scrutinize trios of letter combinations and decide which, if any, spell actual words. This seems to the writer to be a valid test of letter sounds. A test measuring the ability to use a dictionary pronunciation key rounds out the phonics tests. Except for the fact that it utilizes multiple-choice items, it seems to be a valid test of the ability.

Dividing words into syllables is tested by having the students do just that. However, the words would be familiar as sight words to many intermediate grade children and could be divided without the child's possessing knowledge of the principles of syllable division.

The final subtest requires the child to circle affixes in words. This seems to be a valid test and meets most of the criteria for a good diagnostic test.

All things considered, the McCullough Test would be useful with a group of children in intermediate grades, even though the multiple-choice format reduces its effectiveness. In cases where it violates the criteria of a good diagnostic test it is no worse than several others measuring the same abilities.

The McKee Test has been included in the teachers' manuals of the McKee

Reading Series for a number of years and is also available in printed form apart from the manuals. It is designed to evaluate phonics skills such as initial consonants and knowledge of vowel principles, and some structural analysis skills such as inflectional endings and affixes. It utilizes a multiple-choice format and is thus susceptible to guessing and requires children to listen and choose the response that contains the same initial sound (or syllable), final sound, or medial vowel as the one spoken by the teacher. This ability is, of course, different from that required in actual reading, in which the child is confronted by symbols and must supply sound equivalents.

In a study directed by the writer, 43 poor readers in grades five and six were given the McKee Test along with two individually administered tests: one was a nonsense syllable reading test and the other a specially constructed test. The latter utilized words from the Dolch list and required students to pronounce words constructed by changing one element in a Dolch word to make a new word. The changed element was written in cursive writing so that the form of the new word would be unfamiliar. All three tests tested the same basic elements. It was found that if the nonsense word test was used as a criterion, the McKee Test detected only 13.7 percent of the children's individual weaknesses in phonics. If the Dolch-Changed Element Test was used as a criterion, the McKee detected 16.7 percent of the weaknesses in phonics.

Since the McKee Test detected so few of the potential trouble spots in the word recognition abilities of the children, its use is inadvisable. It might be useful in detecting *group* weaknesses but in view of the fact that it utilizes the multiple-choice format, the word perception weaknesses of poor readers are likely to be inaccurately evaluated by it.

Summary

Standardized diagnostic reading tests are likely to be useful to the classroom teacher, especially as models for the diagnostic procedures to be followed. Ideally such procedures will evaluate *many* aspects of reading and the tests used will need to meet most of several important criteria. Very few batteries that evaluate all the important phases of reading and also meet the criteria of a good test are available. Various published tests have specific strengths and weaknesses and are useful in different ways in different situations. A careful examination of several of the tests is recommended before any test is purchased for use in evaluating the various aspects of reading.

REFERENCES
Tests

1. Bond, Guy L., Theodore Clymer, and Cyril J. Hoyt. *The Developmental Reading Tests*, Silent Reading Diagnostic Tests. Chicago: Lyons and Carnahan, 1955.
2. Botel, Morton. *Botel Reading Inventory*. Chicago: The Follett Publishing Co., 1961, 1962, 1966.
3. Brown, Grace M., and Alice Cottrell. *California Phonics Survey*. Monterey, California: California Test Bureau, 1963.
4. Durrell, Donald. *Durrell Analysis of Reading Difficulty*. New York: Harcourt, Brace and World, 1955.
5. Gates, Arthur I., and Anne S. McKillop. *Gates-McKillop Reading Diagnostic Tests*. New York: Bureau of Publications, Teachers College, Columbia University, 1962.
6. Gray, William S. (Helen M. Robinson, Editor) *Gray Oral Reading Test*. Indianapolis, Ind.: The Bobbs-Merrill Co., Inc., 1963.
7. McCullough, Constance M. *McCullough Word-Analysis Tests*. Boston: Ginn and Company, 1960, 1962.
8. McKee, Paul. *The McKee Inventory of Phonetic Skills*. Boston: Houghton Mifflin Co., 1962.
9. Monroe, Marian. *Monroe Diagnostic Reading Examination*. Chicago: C. H. Stoelting Co., 1928.
10. Spache, George D. *Diagnostic Reading Scales*. Monterey, California: California Test Bureau, 1963.
11. Triggs, Frances, *et al. Diagnostic Reading Test: Upper Level*, (Grade 7-College Freshman Year). Mountain Home, North Carolina: The Committee on Diagnostic Reading Tests, 1952, 1958.

Other References

12. Bond, Guy, and Miles A. Tinker. *Reading Difficulties, Their Diagnosis and Correction*. New York: Appleton-Century-Crofts, Inc., 1967.
13. Harris, Albert J. *How to Increase Reading Ability*. New York: David McKay Co., 1961.
14. Shedd, Charles. "Specific Perceptual Motor Disabilities," speech delivered at NDEA Institute in Reading, University of Kentucky, July 29, 1966.
15. Thorndike, E. L. "Reading as Reasoning: A Study of Mistakes in Paragraph Reading," *Journal of Educational Psychology, 8* (June 1917), 323-332.
16. Trella, Thaddeus M. "What Do Diagnostic Reading Tests Diagnose?" *Elementary English, 43* (April 1966), 370-372.
17. Zintz, Miles V. *Corrective Reading*. Dubuque, Iowa: William C. Brown, 1966.

ROBERT A. MCCRACKEN

WESTERN WASHINGTON STATE COLLEGE

7. The Informal Reading Inventory as a Means of Improving Instruction

TEACHERS give informal reading inventories every time they make a reading assignment, every time they give a test, every time they discuss with children what has been read. The informal reading inventory can lead to improved instruction, but using an informal reading inventory does not automatically improve instruction. For an informal reading inventory to affect improvement in teaching a teacher must know what an informal reading inventory is; how to administer, record and evaluate the results; and how to use the results.

This paper is organized into two sections. The first section defines an informal reading inventory, tells how to administer it, and presents objective standards for evaluating the results. The second section concerns the use of informal reading inventory results in the classroom.

What Is Informal Reading Testing?

An informal reading test or inventory is a nonstandardized reading test. A child's abilities in reading are tested using excerpts from a graded set of books or a single text. The child reads these excerpts orally and/or silently and the teacher obtains samples of the child's reading performance at each book level. The child's reading performance is evaluated against predetermined standards.

One basic purpose in informal testing is to determine if a text which the teacher wishes to use is too hard to read, about right in reading difficulty, or too easy for a given child. (A book which is rated as too easy in reading difficulty may be used because its content is important, but it would not be used as a text from which to teach a student to read.) A second basic purpose of an informal reading test is to determine the book level or levels at which each child can be instructed in reading. These two purposes are not in conflict. This second purpose, however, usually requires more time and more testing.

The word *informal* may be misleading. The testing procedures and standards are set and fairly formal. *Informal* means that the testing is non-standardized in the technical sense of test construction and administration. *Informal* does not mean relaxed or subjective.

Informal reading testing presumes that reading achievement reflects a developmental growth pattern similar to growth in physical weight, height, shoe or shirt size. One does not need to know the size of a shirt to determine if it fits a child. One puts the shirt on the child and observes if the shoulders are too broad or too small, if the sleeves are a reasonable length, if the neck can be buttoned, etc. One can judge if a shirt size is proper because one knows how a shirt should fit. As a matter of convenience (perhaps necessity in our society) shirt sizes have been given numbers and manufacturers use the same standards for marking shirt sizes. However, one rarely measures the length of a child's arm or the size of his neck to determine his shirt size. One uses the shirt as the measuring stick. If a size fourteen shirt is too tight in the neck, one tries on a size fifteen, etc. When a size fourteen shirt becomes too small because a child is growing, the next larger size is bought. This approach is informal testing of shirt size, and the procedures used are fairly regular. One accepts and uses these fitting procedures because they work.

Informal reading testing does the same thing with books; it helps a teacher decide whether or not a book is the right size for a child, and it determines which book sizes are acceptable for instruction in reading. In informal reading testing one tries on a book for size.

Figure 1 presents this concept diagrammatically. Note that in this example the child can wear a size 12, 13, or 14 shirt even though size 13 is the best fit. Note that the child needs instruction in reading from book sizes 6, 7, 8, and 9. With instructional help he can read from all these levels. The best book for instruction is book 7, but books are not too easy until book 5 level and below nor too hard until book 10 level and above. A child's instructional level in reading usually is more than a single book level although we sometimes say that a student's instructional level is the midpoint of his instructional reading range or the level from which he can be instructed best.

How Is an Informal Reading Test Administered?

Betts (*1*), Cooper (*3*), Durrell (*4*), Harris (*5*), Johnson and Kress (*6*), Russell (*7*), Sheldon (*8*), and others have described informal reading inventories. Basically the method used in administering an informal reading inventory is as follows:

1. The child is asked to read both orally and silently from a graded series of books, usually a basal reading series. The child begins at a

Figure 1
Shirt Size and Book Size Measurements

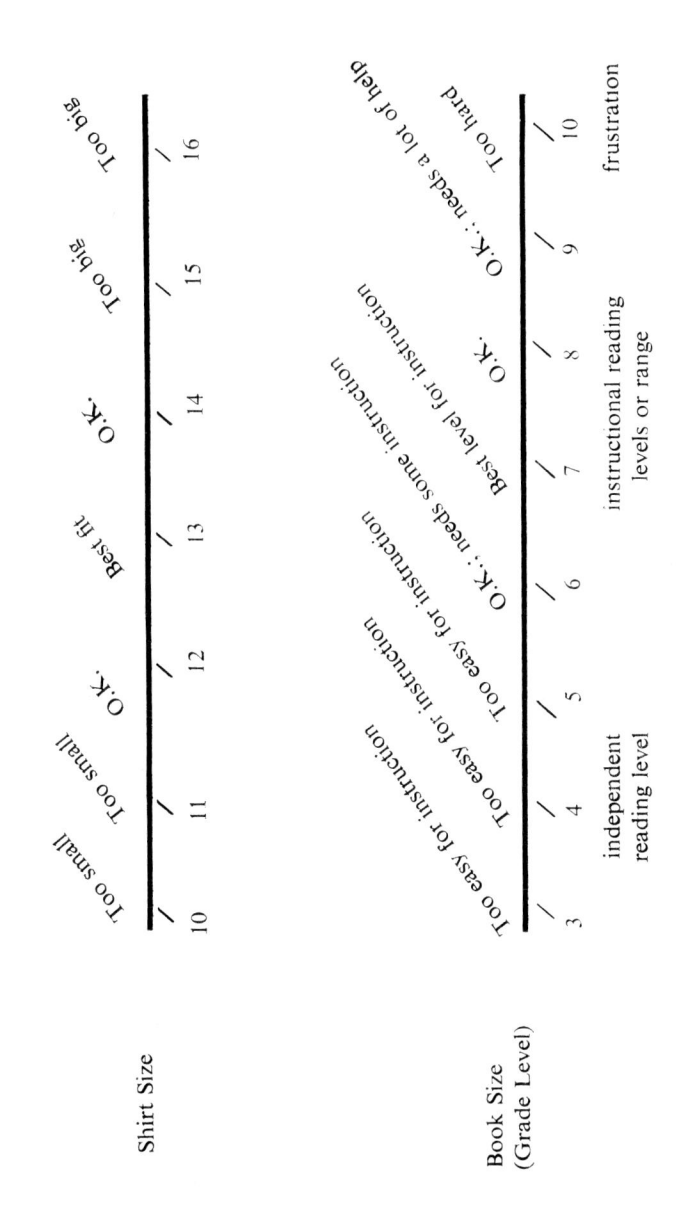

Shirt Size

Too small	Too small	O.K.	Best fit	O.K.	Too big	Too big
10	11	12	13	14	15	16

Book Size
(Grade Level)

Too easy for instruction	Too easy for instruction	Too easy for instruction	O.K.: needs some instruction	Best level for instruction	O.K.	O.K.: needs a lot of help	Too hard
3	4	5	6	7	8	9	10

independent reading level — instructional reading levels or range — frustration

level which is easy and the testing proceeds upward until the material is too difficult for him to read. Usually one selection is read orally and one silently at each book level.
2. As the child reads orally, the manner in which he reads is recorded. Almost any deviation from completely fluent reading is counted as an oral reading error.
3. After reading each selection, the child's comprehension is checked by having the child retell the story, by asking the child questions, or both.

A comprehensive informal reading inventory would include tests for the following abilities:

(a) to read orally without error
(b) to pronounce vocabulary in context (this is the percentage of words which a child recognizes when he is reading orally)
(c) to pronounce words in isolation, usually from word lists of *new* or *difficult* words introduced at a given book level
(d) to demonstrate comprehension of material read orally and material read silently (oral responses, written responses, responses to questions, and free responses)
(e) to define words in context, a part of comprehension which is frequently overlooked
(f) to answer questions which require going beyond recall, a part of comprehension which is frequently overlooked
(g) to record speed of oral reading
(h) to record speed of silent reading
(i) to reread orally or silently to find the answer to a question missed in a comprehension check
(j) to skim new material to find the answer to a question
(k) to skim material which has already been read to find proof of an answer
(l) to apply appropriate study skills to text material, such as locating information using an index, using a glossary to determine word meaning, etc.

Standards for Evaluating an Informal Reading Test

The reading achievement of the child at each book level is evaluated as being *independent reading level*, *instructional reading level*, and *frustration level*. The terms are almost self-explanatory.

The *independent reading level* is the highest book level at which a child can read without assistance. His comprehension is excellent, his reading is fluent, and he is completely comfortable when reading.

The *instructional reading level* is the book level (usually levels) at which the child can profit from and needs instruction from a teacher. A child's instructional reading level is almost always two or three book levels and sometimes six or seven.

Frustration level is the lowest book level at which the child cannot be expected to learn to read even with excellent instruction.

Figure 2 lists the standards for evaluating a child's achievement on an informal reading inventory. These standards are suggested as ones a teacher should use in learning how to use an informal reading inventory. The standards are based upon those found in the literature but are more detailed and more objective. For example, 75 to 90 percent is a common standard of comprehension for instructional level and 50 percent and below, for frustration. The literature is not clear about what to do with comprehension between 50 and 75 percent. A teacher who is experienced in the administration of an informal reading inventory should make subjective judgments when determining a child's reading levels. However, a teacher who is not experienced in administering an informal reading inventory should not make subjective judgments. Subjective judgments made by a teacher inexperienced with an informal reading inventory usually rate the child too high, placing him in frustration level for instruction.

The following rules are applied in evaluating a child's reading performance in using the standards in Figures 2 and 3. These are applied at each book level or to each book which is checked.

1. To rate a child's reading as independent, *EVERY* test score must rate as independent level. If seven scores rate as independent and one rates as instructional, the performance is rated as instructional. This classification means that the child is almost, but not quite, at the cutting point for independence. (Note the continuum in Figure 1.)
2. If *ONE* test score rates as frustration, the child's reading is rated as frustration regardless of the quality of the other scores.
3. If one-half or more of the scores fall under the questionable half of instructional level, the performance is rated as frustration level.
4. If a child makes a better score when reading from a higher book level, the higher score is accepted as valid and the lower score is disregarded. For example, if after silent reading a child comprehends 95 percent of the material read at sixth reader level, but only 60 percent at the fourth or fifth reader level, one would have to conclude that the 60 percent score was invalid.

Counting Oral Reading Errors

There is some disagreement in the professional literature in the enumerating and the counting of oral reading errors. There is some disagreement

Figure 2
Standards for Evaluating Achievement on an Informal Reading Inventory

Skill	FRUSTRATION LEVEL	INSTRUCTIONAL LEVEL (questionable)	INSTRUCTIONAL LEVEL (definite)	INDEPENDENT LEVEL
vocabulary (pronouncing in isolation)		below 50%	50% to 89%	90% to 100%
(pronouncing in context)*	94% or less	95% to 96%	97% to 98%	99% to 100%
errors**	1/10 or less	1/11 to 1/19	1/20 to 1/39	1/40 or better
comprehension and defining vocabulary in context	50% or less	51% to 69%	70% to 89%	90% to 100%
Speed	Silent reading speed definitely slower than oral (15 or more words per minute)	Any speed less than the listed minimums, or when oral and silent reading speeds are about the same.	Speed exceeds suggested minimums and silent speed exceeds oral speed by 15 or more words per minute.	Speed exceeds suggested minimums and silent speed is double oral speed.

*Percentage of words known when reading a paragraph or story. *Unknown words* are generally those which the examiner has to pronounce for the child.

**This is an error ratio—the number of errors: the number of words read; e.g., three errors in reading 96 words yields a ratio of 1/32 (instructional level), seven errors in 96 words yields a ratio of 1/13 (instructional level), twelve errors in 96 words yields a ratio of 1/8 (frustration level).

Figure 3
Suggested Minimum Speeds of Reading in Basal Readers

Book level	Words per minute	
	Oral	Silent
Primer - 1^2	60	60
2^1 & 2^2	70	70
3^1 & 3^2	90	120
4	120	150
5	120	170
6	150	245
7	150	300

about which errors are important enough to be counted. There are two considerations in determining what to count: (a) the error counting should be objective so that examiners can agree, and (b) the error counting should be easy enough to learn so that lengthy or highly specialized training or skill is not necessary. The following lists the oral errors to be noted in scoring an informal reading inventory. This list is based upon experience in training classroom teachers to administer informal reading inventories.

1. repetition—the repeating of a word or phrase
2. substitution—saying one word instead of the one in print
3. addition—inserting word or words or adding an affix
4. pronunciation—the examiner pronounces an unknown word for the child
5. omission—omitting a word, a phrase, or an affix
6. mispronunciation—saying a word in a manner which is definitely incorrect and not a result of defective speech or colloquial pronunciation
7. punctuation—phrasing in which the punctuation is definitely misread or added. Ignoring punctuation is not an error.

It was found one could get reliable counting of errors if one eliminated *hesitations* as an error category. Hesitations were not scored reliably; classroom teachers could not agree whether the hesitations had occurred.

One found that classroom teachers could not always agree on the classification of some types of errors. One did not seem able to teach which errors were significant and which were not—indicating that a criterion for errors which just counted the number of errors was best.

It was also found that the error pattern seemed related to level of difficulty and not to the type of difficulty the child might be having. For example, a good reader in sixth grade will make no errors when reading orally from a second or third reader. He begins to make repetitions as the difficulty of the material increases to fourth and fifth grade levels.

In the sixth and seventh grade level selections, the good reader begins to make substitutions and additions, but he will correct these errors. At the eighth and ninth grade levels, he begins to meet unknown words, to make omissions, and to mispronounce words without correcting these errors. Finally, he waits for assistance in pronouncing words in tenth grade level material and in materials above this level.

As the level of difficulty increases, the beginning errors persist; but proportionately they are less. This finding seemed also to indicate that the counting of the number of errors is more important than is the classification.

It has been argued that self-corrected errors should not be counted. However, a child who makes numerous errors and self-corrects all of them soon becomes frustrated through lack of success and through the slowness of intake of ideas. Self-correction cuts down reading rate. Slow reading rates are associated with frustration, with students *not* reading, and with students *not* doing assignments even though they seem able to do so.

Each type of error is counted equally; a repetition is counted as one error, an omission is counted as one error, or a word which has to be pronounced by the teacher is counted as one error. The type of error may have significance in determining what the student needs to be taught; but in determining instructional reading level the number of errors, not the kinds, is what is important. (The author suggests that diagnostic analysis of error pattern is valid only within the instructional range.)

To make error counting objective and precise, six rules are used:

1. Count only one error at any one place in the reading. Many times a student will make more than one type of error at one point in the story. For example, a student may omit a difficult word, reread (repetition) and mispronounce the omitted word, reread again (another repetition) and pronounce the word correctly. All of this would be counted as one error.
2. Count as one error if a student corrects an error, with or without repeating other words.
3. Count as one error the omission of more than one word of consecutive print.
4. Count as one error the addition of two or more words consecutively.

5. Count as one error if the child makes a second error caused by his forcing grammatical agreement. For example, a child who substitutes *he* for *they* will probably add an *s* to the verb, reading *he wants* for *they want*. The same thing happens when a male proper name is read as female. Later, the pronoun *he* is sometimes read as *she*, or *him* as *her*.
6. Count as one error the mispronouncing of a proper name or difficult word if the word appears more than once in a 100 to 150 word selection and is mispronounced two or more times. For example, students will sometimes read *Bill* as *Billy* consistently. Count as one error if a proper name has two or more words in it and both are mispronounced. Count errors on simple words each time they occur. For example, if *a* is substituted for *the* three times, count three errors.

Note on Frustration Level

When a book or story is at frustration level for a student, this means that the book or story is so hard that the student cannot learn to read from the book even with help; it means that he will not read from the book if assigned to work alone in it; it means that if he is forced to try to read, he will fail and be frustrated in his attempts. A student does not have to exhibit all of the characteristics or symptoms of frustration to have reached frustration. One inability or several partial inabilities are sufficient to cause frustration. Frustration level usually is considerably higher than independent level; that is, a child meets frustration in books which are much harder in reading level than the level of the books which he can read independently.

Adults can experience frustration level by reading a technical text in a discipline in which they are ignorant, reading a simple fairy tale in a foreign language in which they have only a minimum competence, or by reading a mature novel or adult text while holding the book upside down. It is sometimes necessary to read for five minutes or more to become frustrated. It is very hard to be frustrated in thirty to sixty seconds even though all the characteristics of frustration may be evident. When reading from the technical text in an unknown discipline, the frustration will probably come from inability to understand the material. When reading from a simple story in a foreign language, the frustration will probably come from inability or uncertainty in how to pronounce the words. When reading from the adult story while holding the material upside down, the frustration will probably come from making and correcting numerous mistakes. Each one of these inabilities or difficulties is sufficient to cause personal frustration and an unwillingness to read if the reading is carried on for half an hour or more. The author strongly recommends that all beginning reading teachers force themselves to experience frustration in reading by trying all or at least one of these.

Note that frustration is not a matter of averaging. A perfect comprehension score does not offset inability to read orally; the ability to read fluently orally does not offset 30 to 40 percent comprehension. It is perfectly reasonable to expect perfect comprehension of a fairy tale printed in a foreign language, but the inability to "read" is frustration.

Note on Reliability and Validity of Informal Testing

Does informal testing give a fair sample of how a student will perform in a whole book? One of the beauties of informal testing is that it can be repeated using different pages when a teacher is in doubt. If a teacher is uncertain about error recording, if a teacher is uncertain whether a particular paragraph is typical of the book in which it is found, she can select another section and repeat the testing. For most students the following guides will ensure valid testing:

1. Select paragraphs or passages which are 100 to 200 words in length. Longer passages do not seem to be necessary, and they add to the testing time. A total of 100 words is ample for oral reading.
2. Select passages which can be comprehended without special knowledge of what has preceded or what comes next. Select passages which have something to be comprehended. Some 100 word samples convey little meaning.
3. Thirty seconds of elapsed time usually are sufficient for oral reading although this period may not cover 100 words. If a child is struggling through a passage of 150 words and is less than halfway through in thirty seconds, there is no need to continue to prove that he is frustrated. If a child is frustrated on the first three or four sentences of a story, he will remain frustrated. A teacher should stop the testing and shift to a lower level.
4. Be careful in selecting stories or passages from the first unit of a basal reading book since the first unit sometimes is a review of the previous level.

With short passages it is improbable that any student will be frustrated when asked to read (provided the teacher pronounces the unknown words). Since testing is sampling of the student's reading achievement, one must remember that the amount of frustration encountered in reading for one or two minutes of testing will be multiplied when a student is expected to read from a text for 15 minutes or more. A little bit of frustration, the small signs, encountered during testing should be accepted as indicative of frustration.

In the same way, the small amount of instruction apparently needed in short passages near a student's independent reading level should not be ignored. These small instructional needs are also multiplied as the amount to be read is increased. If a student needs help in pronouncing or understanding one word in 50 running words in a story, a teacher would have 40 words to teach in a 2000 word story. Teaching 40 words before or while a story is being read would be an impossible teaching task.

Note on Speed

Informal testing can be conducted without measuring speed of reading. Speed of reading, however, seems to be a highly sensitive measure of the difficulty a child is encountering while reading. Speed of reading is measured in words per minute. Words per minute may be a misnomer. A better name might be *ideas perceived per minute*. The number of ideas in a paragraph seems to be related to the number of words so that measures of speed of reading may be measures of ideas perceived per minute.

A child will not read for any length of time if his intake of ideas is so small per minute that he is bored or frustrated by lack of progress. The use of speed seems justified when selecting library books for free reading or textbooks for daily instruction, particularly for those children who can read but don't or won't. Speed is a good predictor of frustration of longer passages and a good predictor of which children are able to do their homework assignments fast enough to bother doing them regularly. Failure to meet the suggested minimum standards predicts that a child will not do an assignment or read a book; surpassing predicts that he will, if he measures at least at instructional level otherwise. Knowing whether a child will read a book or do an assignment is probably as important as knowing if the child can.

Speed testing is the easiest of the informal testing measures to make objectively. Examiners may disagree concerning error count or comprehension percentage, but there is little disagreement about rate if a stopwatch is used.

To evaluate speed it is usually necessary to have measures of both oral and silent reading speeds. The difference between oral speed and silent speed determines the evaluation as much as the speeds themselves. The measurement of silent speed should be accompanied by a measurement of comprehension because a high silent speed without comprehension is meaningless. The frustration caused by low comprehension takes care of this disparity.

Note that speed, by itself, cannot cause a child's reading to be rated as frustration level unless the child's silent speed is significantly less (15 words per minute or more) than his oral speed at the same level. This circumstance occurs rarely. Speed can contribute to a frustration rating since speeds below the minimum standards are scored under the questionable part of instructional level. Oral and silent speed are counted as separate scores when determining if half or more of the child's scores fall under the questionable part of instructional level.

The standards for speed in Figure 3 are minimum standards, not average speeds. Average speeds are well above these minimum standards. The standards are for use at traditional basal reader levels. A teacher may use these with science, social studies, or trade books; but she should be cautious in determining the "basal reader level" of such books. The use of the levels yielded by the Botel Predicting Readability Levels (2) is a good technique. The speed standards are by book level regardless of the child's grade placement. A child reading at a given book level either exceeds or does not exceed the minimum speed standard. He does not pass or fail. His words per minute *must not* be read as a grade level by moving left in the chart from the speed to a book level. The comparisons for oral and silent speed, however, can be used without regard to level.

Using an Informal Reading Inventory to Affect Instruction

In one third grade in a traditional school, basal reading was the adopted program. It was September. Mrs. Smith was the teacher. She had taught fifteen years but she was new to teaching third grade. She asked the reading consultant for help because the children in her reading groups were not responding well. She had inherited three reading groups from the second grade and had shifted one child.

Her top group had six children reading from a 3-2 level basal reader and doing the accompanying workbook exercises. The children were a joy but always finished their reading seat-work before the teacher had another activity ready. Her middle group had fourteen children reading from a 3-1 level and doing a good job. Her bottom group had eight children trying to read from a 3-1 level basal reader. They could not work independently even after instruction. They had trouble with silent reading, needed constant help when reading orally around the circle, and rarely got better than 50 percent the first time they did their workbook exercises. The teacher was using the same techniques with each group, techniques which seemed to work only with the middle group.

The reading consultant administered an informal reading inventory. The reason for Mrs. Smith's difficulties was apparent from the results. All six pupils in the top group were independent at level 3-2. All fourteen pupils in the middle group needed instruction at third reader level. All eight pupils in the bottom group were frustrated with 3-1 level material. Mrs. Smith and the second grade teacher had recognized individual differences, knew how to conduct informal testing without realizing it, but did not know how to record or evaluate the results.

TABLE 1
SHOE SIZE OF 28 THIRD GRADE CHILDREN IN SEPTEMBER

Size		Number of Pupils
7 - 8	👞	1
5 - 6	👞 👞 👞 👞 👞	5
4	👞 👞 👞 👞	4
3	👞 👞 👞 👞 👞	5
2	👞 👞 👞 👞 👞 👞	6
1	👞 👞 👞 👞 👞 👞	6
12	👞	1

TABLE 2
BOOK SIZE OF 28 THIRD GRADE CHILDREN IN SEPTEMBER

Book Size		Number of Pupils
6 and above	📖 📖	2
5	📖 📖	2
4	📖 📖	2
3^2	📖 📖 📖 📖 📖 📖	6
3^1	📖 📖 📖 📖 📖 📖 📖 📖	8
2	📖 📖 📖 📖 📖	5
1	📖 📖 📖	3

Mrs. Smith saw the implications, but she was worried. The children would not like to be treated differently. The low group would be embarrassed by an easy book. They had read the 2-2 book last year!

The reading consultant made a chart, reproduced in Table 1. Each child took off his shoe and read his shoe size.

Each child was asked, "Why do you wear that particular shoe size?"

Pupils answered consistently, "Because it fits."

"Why don't you wear a bigger shoe? Don't you want your foot to grow faster?"

"That's crazy," a pupil said. "If my shoe didn't fit, it would hurt my foot or fall off when I run."

The reading consultant and the children talked about shoe sizes and the sequence of numerals indicating sizes. They talked about the impossibility of feet growing to be size 6 without having first been size 5 or size 4. They agreed that feet grow gradually from size 1 to 2, from 2 to 3 to 4, etc., not suddenly. They talked about book size and developed the concept that the numerals on basal readers are sizes, not grade level. They developed the concept that children learn to read book 2 after mastering book 1, book 3 after mastering book 2, etc.

The reading consultant made another chart, reproduced in Table 2. He told the children that he had measured their book sizes just as a shoe salesman might measure their foot sizes. He asked the pupils what their book sizes meant. From the top group came responses such as, "I need a harder book. Our reader is too easy. I've got a big book size." From the bottom group came responses such as, "I knew that book was too hard. I need an easy book. No wonder reading is hard."

Mrs. Smith told the children that many of them were going to shift into different books for reading instruction, that they would work in these books for one week, and that she would then ask them if their books fit. She explained that after the shoe salesman fits the shoe to your foot, he asks you to walk around a bit to see how it feels. After a week's instruction Mrs. Smith was going to ask, "How does your book fit?"

For a week the top group worked in book 4 and was assigned to choose library books for independent reading. The middle group continued reading from 3-1 level. The bottom group worked from a reader for bridging 1-2 and 2-1 levels. The methods of instruction shifted slightly during this first week primarily because the children in the bottom group did not need constant attention.

At the end of the week one boy asked to change. He was the poorest reader in the middle group. He wanted to work in the bottom group. Two of the top group children said that book 4 was, "Awful easy, but better than 3-2."

Some things stand out in this story:

1. *Children recognize and accept individual differences.* Teachers project adult fears when thinking that children are embarrassed by our recognizing that they are *poor* readers. The use of the word *poor* reflects this attitude. No one speaks of a *poor* shoe size. Children frequently are relieved when the teacher recognizes their difficulties. In the same way, adults are relieved when a doctor says, "You have *mal-and-sicitis*. It will take awhile but we can cure it." Compare reactions to this statement and to one in which the doctor says, "I don't think there is anything wrong with you. Just try a little harder to think that you're well."
2. *Children can understand the need for grouping and individual attention.* They accept book size as a concept, and they accept instruction whenever they can succeed. *Poor* readers do not object to *easy, baby* reading books if they are successful in them. *Poor* readers don't want to fail in *easy* materials. If they are going to fail, they want to fail something respectable. Failure at grade level is respectable. It is this reaction to failure in *easy* books which has led teachers to conclude that pupils reject *easy* materials.
3. *A low reading group can work independently much of the time.* The material has to be at their instructional level.

Mrs. Smith had a worry. Won't the children in group one miss the skill program? Obviously not. The children already had mastery of the skill program. Mrs. Smith had another worry. Won't the low reading group be retarded by the lack of challenge? One can infer the answer by observing the top group. The top group came to third grade with mastery of the third grade reading program without ever having been taught from a reader harder than 2-2. Perhaps these children would have been more advanced had they had instruction at higher levels. But one cannot, on the basis of observations of top reading groups, conclude that *challenging* children makes them successful. Our most successful groups are those which have never been challenged much by reading group work. Working at an easy level with high success seems more important than challenge.

This story does not end with three groups in basal readers. The top group expanded into individualized reading without the teacher's being aware of it. Much of the reading instruction shifted to social studies and science. The success of the top group in self-selection led to the middle and bottom groups' having the same privilege. The classroom library was greatly expanded with plenty of easy picture books.

The informal testing led to a closer analysis of individual needs. Mrs. Smith assumed responsibility for continuous diagnostic observation. When a child had difficulty at instructional level, Mrs. Smith could see the difficulty because it was not shrouded with the maze of troubles which abound at frustration level. The able readers moved into projects which occasionally frustrated them, but more often just highlighted instructional needs; inefficient study skills and inefficient, ineffective note-taking stood out.

Mrs. Smith developed a sensitivity to standards of performance so that her instruction took its cue from pupils' performances, not from grade level expectancies. The stumbling of the poor reader group no longer sounded right because that was the way the poor reading groups always sounded. The fluency of the top reading group no longer sounded right when it reflected complete independence with the material. Both Mrs. Smith and the pupils were affected by the use of the informal reading inventory, and so was the teacher of grade four the following year when the pupils did not want to be in the same book and told the teacher why. But that is another story.

The description of another class, a fifth grade with 37 pupils, follows. Mr. Baron wanted to improve his social studies teaching. He had 40 copies of one text, as mandated by the district curriculum. He was doing the best job he could, but found that discipline sometimes was a problem. When discipline was not a problem, the children were apathetic and he had trouble covering the work. Mr. Baron knew about informal testing, although he had never really used it much. With 37 pupils he said he didn't have time to test each child. He already had the grades for the first six weeks of work in social studies: 5 A's, 11 B's, 15 C's, 4 D's, and 2 F's. Mr. Baron said they had tried projects and grouping but it didn't work. He had reverted to reading the text around the room. "At least I know that they have covered the material that way," he said.

Mr. Baron sounds like a teacher you and I don't want in our school. But he is not a poor teacher. He is frustrated. This is the classic syndrome of frustration in reading; the child and the teacher are equally frustrated.

The reading consultant visited Mr. Baron's social studies class for one day and listened to the reading circle. He noted the names of the pupils who were obviously frustrated, those who found the material to be at their independent level, and those who read with instructional competence. The consultant compared his results with Mr. Baron's grades. Much to Mr. Baron's surprise the reading consultant had identified the D and F pupils as frustrated and identified the A students as independent. The reading consultant had rated five others very close to frustration. Mr. Baron admitted that they were really D pupils but he had too many already. Mr. Baron had done his informal testing, although he did not realize it. But what to do?

Space does not permit describing the intervening steps. They are apparent from the results. The informal reading inventory, however, was discussed in a manner similar to that in Mrs. Smith's class.

Two months later Mr. Baron still had 40 basic social studies texts. Mr. Baron worked with his whole class to set purpose. He then read this basic text quickly, precisely, with added but not overwhelming explanation to those students who wanted to listen while 22 other pupils worked with 46 other books and two sets of encyclopedias. Most of the 46 other books were social studies texts. There were only single copies of 35 of them. Each book had been numbered to tell the book size. Each of the 22 children used the index or table of contents, working out page references which augmented the content of the *basic text*.

Two days later the pupils were all reading. The former F students were looking at pictures and reading captions and were reading some of the material from a social studies book labelled with a numeral one. Some A pupils were working in an adult encyclopedia, some with junior and senior high texts, and one pupil was tackling a college text. The pupils were fitting themselves to book levels. Study guides were developed jointly with Mr. Baron from the basic text material. For two days to two weeks pupils read, discussed in groups, collated and wrote, and finally summarized and tested.

Again some things stand out:

1. Pupils willingly accept individual differences and individual treatment.
2. A teacher was unaware that he had even given an I.R.I. and he was therefore unaware of the implications.
3. Poor readers can read independently in content areas.

One problem developed in both of these classes. The pupils soon asked, "Why do we all have the same spelling list? Why are we all at the same place in our arithmetic book?" But these are the problems which teachers know how to solve.

REFERENCES

1. Betts, Emmett A. *Foundations of Reading Instruction.* New York: American Book Company, 1950.
2. Botel, Morton. *Botel Predicting Readability Levels.* Chicago: Follett Publishing Co., 1962.
3. Cooper, J. Louis. "Criteria for Determining Reading Levels and Suitability of Reading Materials," (mimeographed bulletin). Storrs, Conn.: The Reading Study Center, University of Connecticut (undated).
4. Durrell, Donald D. *Improving Reading Instruction.* New York: World Book Company, 1956.
5. Harris, Albert. *How to Increase Reading Ability.* New York: Longmans, Green and Company, 1956, 1961.

6. Johnson, Marjorie Seddon, and Roy Kress. *Informal Reading Inventories.* Newark, Delaware: International Reading Association, 1965.
7. Russell, David, *et al. The Ginn Basic Readers*, Teachers' Manuals. New York: Ginn and Company, 1960, 1961.
8. Sheldon, Wm. D., *et al. The Sheldon Basic Readers*, Teachers' Manuals. Boston: Allyn and Bacon, Inc., 1957, 1958, and 1963.

Frank J. Guszak

UNIVERSITY OF NEW MEXICO

8. Teachers' Questions and Levels of Reading Comprehension

THE Educational Policies Commission (4) stated that "the purpose which runs through and strengthens all other educational purposes—the common thread of education—is the development of the ability to think." Educators at all levels and in all areas have been concerned with achieving this goal. Observers of the educational scene, however, have taken the position that schools are not doing as well as they might in helping children develop various types and levels of thinking.

With specific reference to reading, there has been some evidence that teachers devote considerably more attention to literal comprehension than they do to higher level comprehension abilities. For example, Austin (2) stated that "a rather low cognitive level is sought by the silent checks and comprehension questions that are found in most classrooms." Echoing the same concern, Henry (5) recently lamented that contemporary readers (students) failed to evaluate or to read analytically.

Spurred by these assertions and others, the study described here was initiated to gather data that would shed some light on the emphases given to teaching reading comprehension. Because the oral question appeared to be the prime thinking stimulus of the classroom teacher as she worked in the reading group, the decision was made to view comprehension from the standpoint of teacher questions about reading content. Since questions without responses indicate only partial insights into potential comprehension development, a further decision was made to study the nature of the students' responses to such questions as well as the patternings of teacher-pupil interaction sequences. Specifically, the investigation sought to answer the following questions:

1. What kinds of thinking outcomes are teachers seeking to stimulate with their oral questions about reading content?
2. To what extent are teacher questions about reading content being met with congruent student responses?
3. What questioning strategies are teachers employing in their verbal interactions with readers?*

*The research reported here was supported by the Cooperative Research Program of the Office of Education, U.S. Department of Health, Education, and Welfare.

Subjects for the study were the teachers and pupils in randomly selected second, fourth, and sixth grade classes in a Texas city with a population of approximately 65,000. Four classes at each of the three grade levels made up the sample. Each reading group in the twelve classrooms was observed and recorded over a three-day period. The recordings were transcribed into written protocols and analyzed in accordance with the research questions.

The results are discussed in accordance with the three research questions. Because the results would be relatively meaningless without an understanding of the measuring modes, the first part of each discussion concerns the descriptive instruments.

What Kinds of Thinking Outcomes Are Teachers Seeking to Stimulate With Their Oral Questions About Reading Content?

In order to describe the thinking modes called for by teacher questions, the Reading Comprehension Question-Response Inventory was developed. The inventory contained the following classifications:

Recognition—These questions call upon the students to utilize their literal comprehension skills in the task of locating information from reading context. Frequently, such questions are employed in the guided reading portion of a story, e.g., "What sentence tells how the dog escaped?"

Recall—Recall questions call for students to demonstrate comprehension by the recall of materials previously read. Such activity is primarily concerned with the retrieval of small pieces of factual material although the activity can vary greatly in difficulty. Recall, like recognition, represents a literal comprehension task. An example of a recall question would be the following where the answer to the question is clearly printed in the text, e.g., "What color was Jack's car?"

Translation—Translation questions require the student to give an objective, part-for-part rendering of a communication. As such, the behavior is characterized by literal understandings in that the translator does not have to discover intricate relationships, implications, or subtle meanings. Translation questions frequently call upon students to change words, ideas, and pictures into different symbolic form as illustrated in the following material from Bloom (*3*).

> Translation from one level of abstraction to another, i.e., abstract to concrete, lengthy to brief communication, etc.
>
> Translation from one symbolic form to another, i.e., pictures to verbal descriptions, verbal descriptions to dramatizations.
>
> Translation from one verbal form to another, i.e., non-literal statements (metaphor, symbolism, exaggeration) to ordinary English.

Conjecture—These questions call for a "cognitive leap" on the part of the student as to what will happen or what might happen. As such, the conjecture is an anticipatory thought and not a rationale, e.g., "Do you think he will win the race?"

Explanation—Explanation questions call upon the students to provide a rationale such as the "why" or "how" of a situation. The rationale must be inferred by the student from the context developed or go beyond it if the situation is data poor in terms of providing a rationale. Examples of explanatory responses are substantiations of claims, e.g., "Explain why you think John was the best"; explanations of value positions, e.g., "Why do you think this is the best story we have read?"; conclusions, e.g., "What can you conclude as the reason for Bill's failure?"; main ideas, e.g., "What is the main idea of this story?"

Evaluation—Evaluation questions deal with matters of value rather than matters of fact or inference and are thus characterized by the judgmental quality of worth, acceptability, probability, etc. The following components of this category are adapted from a classification scheme by Aschner and Gallagher (*1*).

- Questions call for a rating—good, bad, true, etc.—on some item—idea, person, etc.—in terms of some scale of values provided by the teacher.
- Questions call for a value judgment on a dimension set up by the teacher. Generally, these are "yes" or "no" responses following questions such as, "Would you have liked Tom for a brother?"
- Questions that develop from conjectural questions when the question is qualified by such probability statements as "most likely."
- Questions that present the pupil with a choice of two or more alternatives and require a choice; e.g., "Who did the better job in your opinion, Mary or Susan?"

Table I reveals that of the total number of teachers' questions collected in the study 56.9 percent were recall and 13.5 percent were recognition, according to the criteria presented in the Reading Comprehension Question-Response Inventory. Moreover, when these two types of literal comprehension questions were combined, they accounted for 70.4 percent of all the questioning activity recorded in the study. This result tends to support the contention that elementary teachers emphasize literal comprehension during reading time.

Table I also shows that evaluation questions, which accounted for 15.3 percent of all questions, were the second most frequent type of questions asked by teachers in the sample. Conceivably, such evidence casts doubt on the position taken by Henry (*5*) who felt that students never evaluated. However, it should be pointed out that the evaluative behaviors exhibited

TABLE I
FREQUENCIES AND PERCENTAGES OF SIX QUESTION TYPES IN GRADES TWO, FOUR, AND SIX

Grade	Recognition f	Recognition %	Recall f	Recall %	Translation f	Translation %	Conjecture f	Conjecture %	Explanation f	Explanation %	Evaluation f	Evaluation %	Total f	Total %
Two	108	12.3	584	66.5	2	.2	50	5.7	33	3.8	101	11.5	878	100
Four	118	16.3	351	48.4	4	.6	50	6.9	54	7.4	148	20.4	725	100
Six	26	10.2	121	47.6	6	2.4	20	7.9	46	8.1	35	13.8	254	100
Total	252	13.5	1056	56.9	12	.6	120	6.5	133	7.2	284	15.3	1857	100

by the students in terms of this category were primarily "yes" or "no" type evaluative statements and not detailed explanations of value positions. In only a few instances were the students asked to defend or clarify their value positions.

Inferential questions, conjecture (6.5 percent) and explanation (7.2 percent), were third in priority and accounted for 13.7 percent of the total number of teachers' questions summarized in Table I. This result would seem to indicate that such questions received minor emphasis in the reading programs observed during the investigation.

Although the finding related to inferential questions was in keeping with the initial hypothesis held by the investigator, the almost complete absence of translation questions, .6 percent of all questions, was unexpected. It appeared that the teachers in the sample placed more emphasis upon the recall of specific details rather than on tasks that required broader responses encompassed by translation as described in the Reading Comprehension Question-Response Inventory.

When the figures presented in Table I are viewed in terms of comparing the three grade levels, it can be seen that the percentage of literal questions decreases as the grade level increases. Such findings would confirm the common notion that upper grade teachers focus more upon varied reading thinking skills because they have greater freedom from the responsibility of developing literal comprehension skills. Presumably, literal comprehension skills are developed in the primary grades and the emphasis shifts to inferential and evaluative in the intermediate grades.

Differences in the number of questions asked at the three grades were also noted when the data were analyzed. Table I shows that in the second and fourth grades the teachers tended to ask nearly three times as many questions as did the teachers in the sixth grade. By way of explanation it appeared that the lower grade teachers asked many questions in an effort to be sure that their students were understanding the many details of their reading assignments.

To What Extent Are Teacher Questions Being Met With Congruent Student Responses?

To ask a question is one thing. To ask a question and have it met with a congruent response is yet another thing. Such thinking lay behind the development of the second research question and the subsequent development of the *congruence-incongruence* idea. Congruence as used here refers to the reciprocity between the intent of the teacher's question and the ability of the student's response to satisfy that intent. Judgments relative

TABLE II
FREQUENCIES AND PERCENTAGES OF QUESTION-RESPONSE CONGRUENCE IN GRADES TWO, FOUR, AND SIX

Grade	Recognition f	%	Recall f	%	Translation f	%	Conjecture f	%	Explanation f	%	Total f	%
Two	35	94.6	520	92.5	1	100.0	39	95.1	20	80.0	615	92.3
Four	57	91.9	297	88.1	1	50.0	43	91.5	43	86.0	441	88.6
Six	16	100.0	76	84.4	4	80.0	16	100.0	37	88.1	149	88.2
Total	108	93.9	893	90.3	6	75.0	98	94.2	100	85.5	1205	90.4

to congruence are relatively easy to make if the judge possesses sufficient knowledge about the referent of the question.

Table II illustrates the frequencies and percentages of congruence in the three grades.

As indicated, teacher questions were met with congruent student responses in 90.4 percent of the cases. A closer inspection of the table reveals that congruence was somewhat higher in the second grade (92.3 percent) than it was in the fourth grade (88.6 percent) or in the sixth grade (88.2 percent). Furthermore, it appears that congruency was largely a function of recall congruency as the total figures in the recall column in Table II correspond rather closely with the total figures. Thus, the higher second grade congruency appears directly related to the high incidence of congruent recall responses in this grade.

Observations by the investigator indicated that the performance of the second grade with respect to congruent recall responses was largely aided by the many specific fact questions that could be answered by a glance at the page or by easy recall. In the upper grades where the reading materials became more complex, the recall task was more difficult for both students and teachers. Therefore, the upper grade teachers had a tendency to accept incongruent responses because they did not have answers to their own questions.

What Questioning Strategies Are Teachers Employing in Their Oral Interactions With Readers?

The investigation revealed that teachers employed two types of questioning strategies as they interacted with readers about reading content. First, they controlled the nature of the exchange relative to each question. Second, in some instances they patterned such individual question-response exchanges into larger wholes.

In order to describe the strategy elements involved in the single question the concept of the Question-Response Unit (QRU) was developed. The QRU represented the boundaries wherein the anatomy of an exchange could be illustrated. As such it contained the following elements: the teacher's initiating question; any subsequent remarks on the part of the teacher that might serve to extend, clarify, or cue subsequent student response; the referent in the reading materials for the question; the way in which the student subsequently dealt with the question; and finally, the phase wherein attention was shifted away from the initiating question. Diagrammatically, the QRU is represented as follows:

Diagram

Initiating Question — Student Responses

Sustaining Remarks

Referent in Reading Content

Response not permitted
Silence—no response offered
Student says, "I don't know"
Incongruent response

Congruence

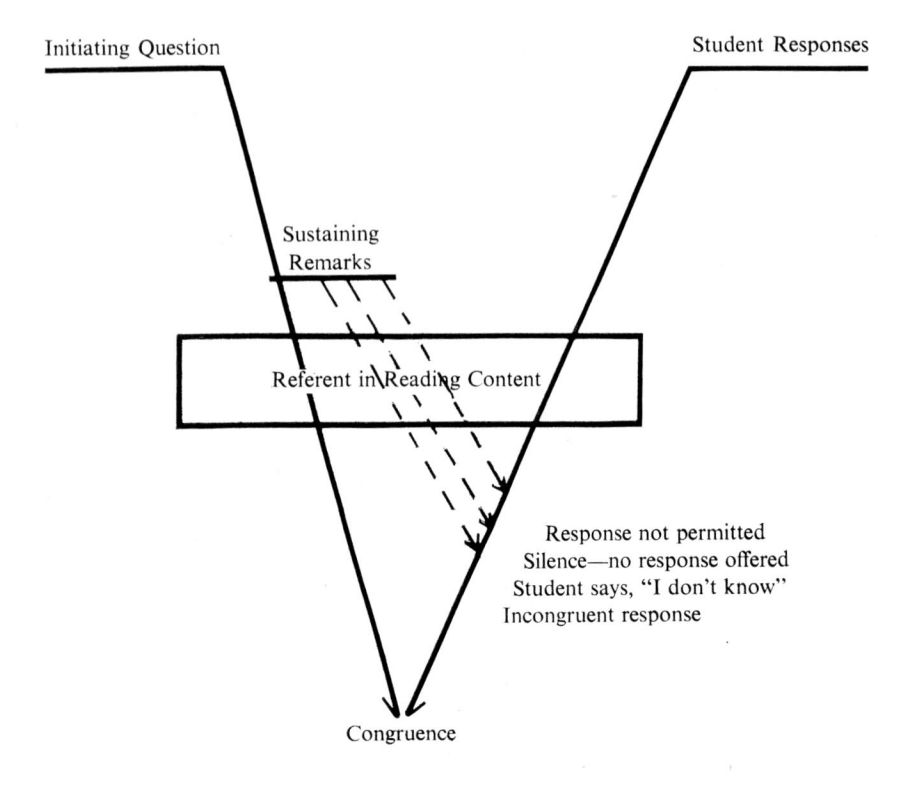

Conceivably, every initiating question can be met by a congruent response on the first response attempt. However, such is not always the case as is illustrated in the diagram. In some instances the teacher may move the focus before a student can respond. In other instances, response time may be allowed but no response may be forthcoming, in which case the teacher may drop the unit or invoke a sustaining statement that will either clarify the question or offer some cues as to the correct response. These examples represent a very small number of alternatives that can happen in the context of a QRU.

In the study, a multitude of QRU patterns were identified. Because so many were seen only in a single instance the decision was made to focus upon those which occurred at least three times. Table III represents a frequency report of such patterns.

It is obvious from Table III that the question followed by a single congruent response (QR+) was the dominant pattern of interaction. Furthermore, observation indicates that the pattern tends to be closely associated with recall questions. Because recall questions were most abundant in the

TABLE III
FREQUENCIES OF QUESTION-RESPONSE UNIT PATTERNS

Patterns	Recognition	Recall	Translation	Conjective	Explanation	Evaluation	Totals
QR+	74	681	4	56	50	189	1054
Q(0) /R+	5	34	0	1	4	2	46
QR−	4	41	0	0	1	0	46
QR-/R+	6	15	0	4	1	1	27
QR+/R+	0	5	0	3	3	4	15
QR+ | R+	1	1	0	2	0	6	10
Q(-)	0	6	1	0	1	1	9
Q(-) /R +	0	5	0	0	0	0	5
Q(0) /(0) /R+	1	2	0	0	1	0	4
QR+ | R−	0	4	0	0	0	0	4
Q(0) /R−/R+	1	2	0	0	0	0	0
Q(0) / (-)	1	1	0	0	1	0	3
Total	93	797	5	66	62	203	1226

Legend

Q   This symbol represents the teacher's initiating question.

R   This capital "R" represents a student response.

/   The diagonal indicates a place wherein the teacher employed a clarifying, extending, or cueing remark. Such verbal actions hold the QRU open.

+ or −   A plus indicates a congruent response while a minus indicates an incongruent one.

(-)   This mark indicates a situation wherein a response was allowed but only silence was heard.

(0)   This mark indicates that the teacher did not allow time for a student response.

| A division line indicates separate responses.

second grade classes, the QR+ pattern was likewise most prominent in the second grade,

A second focus relative to teacher questioning strategies was the concept of the Question-Response Episode. The Question-Response Episode represented a combination of two or more question-response units which tended to be related in the following ways:

Setting Purpose Follow-up—This type of episode would result when a teacher would follow up a "setting purpose" question (S[O]) with a parallel question calling for a response. In other words, the teacher would ask the first question as a guide for the students and then would repeat the question in a manner that would call for response.

Verification—Verification episodes involve questions wherein congruence can be verified by referring to the text. As such, it is the reverse of the previous episode type. In verification episodes, the teacher follows up a student response with a question that calls for the verification or finding of the referent for the response to the previous question.

Justification—This type of episode appears when a teacher calls upon a student to justify his own or somebody else's previous response by the use of explanation. This explanation most frequently follows a judgmental or conjectural response to a previous question.

Judgmental—This episode type refers to situations wherein a teacher will ask for an evaluation of the student response to the preceding question. Thus, judgmental episodes constitute a reversal of the order employed in the justification episodes.

Of the 142 question-response episodes tallied in Table IV, 67 were "setting purpose follow-up" episodes. "Judgmental" episodes represented the least observed episode type as evidenced by six in this category.

TABLE IV

FREQUENCIES OF QUESTION-RESPONSE EPISODES IN GRADES TWO, FOUR, AND SIX

Grade	SP Follow-up	Verification	Justification	Judgmental	Total
Two	26	11	11	3	51
Four	35	14	23	2	74
Six	6	8	2	1	17
Totals	67	33	36	6	142

Each episode represented in Table IV included two question-response units. Thus, the 142 question-response episodes accounted for 284 of the 1857 total units identified in the study.

Conclusions

Although the size of the sample for the study prevents the extensive generalization of its results, the following conclusions regarding the sample may characterize a larger population.

1. The teachers in the sample dwelt on literal comprehension to the neglect of inferential and evaluative dimensions. Not only did the teachers relegate higher reading-thinking skills to a minor role, but they also tended to work at the lowest level of literal comprehension by asking many recall questions about minute facts. Rarely did the teachers build translation questions that called for large segments of literal meaning.

   The root of the problem seemed to be the teacher's lack of understanding of a basic structure of reading-thinking skills. While the manuals for the texts used in the study had structures and suggested questions at various levels, it was evident that teachers did not understand such structures and did not see the relevancy of the questions presented in the manuals. Thus, it seems imperative that textbooks provide teachers with a manageable framework for understanding reading-thinking skills and a means for developing such skills.

2. The high incidence of incongruent units indicated that the teachers were accepting incongruent responses as congruent. It seems very obvious that such a practice cannot develop careful reading-thinking skills. When teachers ask for answers which they do not, themselves, possess and subsequently accept incorrect responses as correct, they are perpetuating habits of inattention and careless thought.

3. The basic questioning strategy of the teachers in the study can be characterized as a "one-shot QR+ pattern" about a recall outcome. As indicated by the pattern, the question is so simple that the student achieves the correct response on the first try. Probably such a pattern is more dangerous than is the incidence of accepting incongruent responses because it encourages readers to scout for the trivial facts that fit this questioning mode. Consequently, children are programmed into such narrow channels of thinking that they cannot or will not employ the reading-thinking abilities and skills of the reflective reader. This narrow pattern of questioning can be broken by thorough understandings of the varied reading-thinking skills, as well as the idea that

a single, correct response is not always desirable. Indeed, at times there should be a multitude of responses to a single question in order that varied viewpoints might be generated and developed.
4. Seldom did the teachers avail themselves of opportunities to employ episodic strategies. Rather, they tended to utilize the question as a free-standing item when, with a minimum of effort, they could have related one question to another. The most alarming finding was the one that indicated that the teachers called for a considerable number of "yes" or "no" value statements from students but subsequently neglected to ask the students to defend their dichotomous positions. Such a practice seems conducive to the development of a narrow individual if that individual is permitted to make frequent verbal value judgments without supporting statements. With a knowledge of the means of relating questions to one another, it seems that teachers could easily employ strategies that would challenge students to think more deeply about their reading materials.

Implications

Attention has long been given to the question as a stimulator of thought. Many appear to recognize the importance of questioning but few have taken specific steps in teacher education to assist prospective teachers and experienced teachers in acquiring knowledge about the kinds of questions they can ask. In terms of reading comprehension, the reading teacher has been given some rather vague notions about ways of soliciting literal comprehension, interpretation, and critical reading in pupils; but he has not been given sharp classifications or concrete situations in which to practice these techniques. Hopefully, the Reading Comprehension Question-Response Inventory and any reading material offer to the student or teacher the opportunity to practice his skill and to develop a useful framework for subsequent practice in the classroom.

By demonstrating that teachers most frequently solicit recall responses the current study has shown the increasing need for attention to other types of thinking in reading instruction. The dramatic finding is the revelation that the single recall solicitation followed by the single congruent recall response (SR+) is the dominant interaction pattern. From this combination it is apparent that teachers utilizing such solicitation activities are conditioning pupil thinking to the point that they will respond with a simple fact. The teacher insures congruence by choosing only those things that will generally be answerable on a single try. Conceivably, teachers should solicit in ways wherein responses may not be congruent on the initial effort or where numerous congruent responses may be offered (conjecture). If highly stimulating inferential solicitations are developed, they may sustain wide response in such a fashion that the abbreviated SR+ pattern becomes an elongated (SR+R R+R+/R−/R+ /R+/R+). For the elongated pattern which generates thought, the teacher must learn to play the new role of the individual who keeps the question open and on the track with timely clarifying, cueing, and extending acts. Too, he must learn to handle the incongruent response in such a manner that it does not defeat its author or subsequent respondents.

Generated from the SR+ pattern is a phenomenon which may be referred to as the "one shot" solicitation pattern. This phenomenon refers to the findings indicating that teachers do not relate questions to one another in larger wholes but tend, for the most part, to solicit in one-shot sequences. To break the one-shot pattern, teachers at all levels should study the patterning concepts embodied in the Solicitation-Response Episode framework. They should be helped to see the importance of asking questions to establish purposes for reading and then to follow up such questions. For example pupils may well be asked to go to the context to verify responses. One of the most distressing teacher practices is that of asking students to choose one side of a value dimension structured by a teacher solicitation and then to be released from the obligation of having to support their value position in some logical manner.

Teachers who are aware of patterns other than "recall SR- one-shot" pattern can substantially alter their verbal solicitation-response interaction with students. They can learn this procedure by applying techniques suggested by the conceptual framework of the major instruments described earlier. This framework can be applied at the preservice and in-service teacher education levels. Both groups could then apply their knowledge to the development of questions and questioning strategies which can help students to acquire a variety of thinking skills in and through reading.

REFERENCES

1. Aschner, Mary June, James J. Gallagher, Joyce M. Perry, Sibel S. Afsar, William Jenne, and Helen Farr. *A System for Classifying Thought Processes in the Context of Classroom Verbal Interaction*. Champaign, Illinois: Institute tor Research on Exceptional Children, 1965.
2. Austin, Mary C., and Coleman Morrison. *The First R: The Harvard Report On Reading in Elementary Schools*. New York: The Macmillan Co., 1964.
3. Bloom, Benjamin S. (Ed.) *Taxonomy of Educational Objectives: Handbook I: Cognitive Domain*. New York: David McKay Company, 1956.
4. Educational Policies Commission. *The Central Purpose of American Education*. Washington, D. C.: National Education Association, 1961.
5. Henry, Jules. "Reading for What?" *Teachers College Record*, LXV (October 1963).

LYMAN C. HUNT, JR.

UNIVERSITY OF VERMONT

9. Evaluation Through Teacher-Pupil Conferences

THE PURPOSE here is to delineate the personal approach to evaluation—an approach which any teacher can employ in her own classroom setting. This approach to evaluation is predicated on certain principles and definitions. One basic principle: Any teacher armed with the proper questions and oriented to the appropriate observations can better evaluate a child's reading through a series of individual conferences than through any other approach. To support this bold assertion the following operational definition of reading is presented. *Reading* in the best sense of the word is what the *child* does with *his* book. Teaching reading then becomes all that the teacher does to facilitate the interaction between the child and *his* book. Evaluation of the child's reading becomes a matter of precision in observation, of how much the book matters to the child, and of the depth and breadth of response the child makes to the ideas in *his* book. Appropriately, the teacher is the one to make the judgment about the total effect reading has on each child's learning and growing.

To set the stage for this sort of evaluation, the teacher must provide sufficient time for children to read books—books which have been freely chosen and which are willingly read. When the day arrives that the teacher can stand aside and observe every child deeply engrossed in silent reading of his own book, then she can engage in the highly personal evaluation of the individual conference.

The individual teacher-pupil conference provides for maximum impact in terms of teacher-learner interaction. To state a second basic principle, each conference time is both a teaching and an evaluation session. It is through keen observation during the conference that the teacher learns more about a child's reading than through any other single evaluation activity.

By contrast, in the typical ability group setting little undivided time can be allocated to each individual within the group. The teacher is too nervously concerned with the pacing of the whole group and the impatience of other children who are waiting turns. Group momentum is lost if too much special concern is directed toward one individual within the group. Constant conflict arises between giving attention to one yet attending to the wishes of all the others.

A misconception can easily arise at this point. Much evaluation can be accomplished within small group settings other than the ability group situation. Discussing books with children in small groups, when each child brings his own book, contributes much to the total evaluation effort. In addition, holding periodic discussions on progress being made in reading within the whole class adds substantially to overall evaluation. But the one-to-one teacher-pupil conference is indispensable to the best evaluation of reading performance. Through the summation of impressions gained from all reading situations, the teacher really knows each child for the reader that he is.

The personal approach to evaluation of each child is truly a many-sided affair. The keen, observant teacher watches and appraises from many angles. Thus, the following evaluative situations will be described insofar as space permits: (a) the individual teacher-pupil conference with emphasis on the general teacher-pupil conference and the diagnostic teacher-pupil conference; (b) the small group conference; and (c) the total class conference.

The Individual Teacher-Pupil Conference

The teacher-pupil conference is a highly personal matter; thus, inevitably it is an expression of the two persons involved—the teacher and the pupil. The personality of each colors the situation and, in essence, determines the nature of each conference. No one can prescribe exactly what the teacher should say or do. No one should try. The teacher's personality must dominate and determine the pattern and tone for every conference. She is the constant factor, she is always there. On the other hand, the child's personality is the independent variable—the unpredictable ingredient which makes each conference a unique and highly individual teaching-learning experience. The child's reactions and responses to the books and materials being read become the focal point of the teacher-pupil conference, the object of the teacher's observations.

The intent here is to present generalized patterns which typically occur during conference time. Hopefully, models or types can be established to aid teachers in developing skill in handling the conference situations and yet caution each teacher once more that she must be the prime mover of the conference. She must be instrumental in developing the conference into a successful activity. Her art and power of asking questions and responding instantly and intelligently to the child's reactions with more questions are the key to success. It is her responsibility to initiate the action; most children will take off from the stimulus which she provides.

Two models for the individual conference will be developed. The first type is more general in nature and suits any regular classroom situation; the second is more specific and pertains in particular to assessing unusual difficulties which children frequently encounter in reading.

The General Teacher-Pupil Conference

The conference time should not be a time for merely assuring one's self that the child has read and remembered every part of every page of his book. Undoubtedly, the worst command that a teacher can give in conference time is "Tell me about your book" or, phrased differently, "Tell me everything you can remember about your book." Nor is the conference the time to elicit answers to a long list of factual questions about every part of each book. The conference time is not the place where the teacher needs to sit with an individual child and listen to him read long passages orally, or to record the many mistakes he makes by seeing how many words he does not know. By contrast, the conference time must give the child an opportunity to reveal his strength as a reader through his personal responses to the book which he has chosen to read. The teacher's task is to assess the reader rather than the content of the book which has been read.

Perceptive, penetrating questions can reveal relatively quickly the depth of a child's reading. It is of fundamental importance that the teacher have a repertoire of questions at the tip of her tongue. Having several broad areas in mind within which questions can be framed is the key. This task is best accomplished by grouping into three major categories questions most frequently asked within the conference: (a) appropriateness of the book, (b) appreciation of the book, and (c) values gained from the book (*1*).

Appropriateness of the book. These questions are designed to determine the appropriateness of the choice of a particular book by a particular child.

1. Why did you choose this particular book?
2. Was this a good choice? or, Was this a good book for you to read?
3. Could you tell what was happening all the time?
4. Was this book hard? or, Was it easy for you to read?
5. What made it hard? or, What made it easy?
6. Were there places where you got mixed up? or, Were there places where you didn't understand? and if so, How did you straighten yourself out?
7. Would you choose the same kind or a different kind of book next?

8. Did you want to keep on reading? or, Did you have to force yourself to finish the book?

Answers to such questions give real clues about how wise a choice the child has made. The function of the teacher is to help each child make the best possible choices. But the final choice rests with the child. The choice should be his unless it is clear that he cannot handle this degree of freedom.

Appreciation of book. These questions are so structured that the degree of appreciation of the book is revealed. An effort is made to have the reader place the book on a continuum of best liked to least liked of the several books which have been read recently.

1. What type of a book are you reading (type of literature)?
2. Was this a good book? If "Yes," How good?
3. Was this not a good book? If "No," How poor?
4. What made this a good (or poor) book? What was it about the book that made it good?
5. How close to the top (or bottom) of your list would you put it (compared to other books read recently)?
6. Was this the best (or worst) book you have read (compared to all the books read)?
7. How much do you usually like books of this type?
8. Do you think you would like to read this book again?
9. Would you like to read other books by this same writer?
10. Who else in the class would like to read this book?
11. Do you want to share your book with the class?

A reader must learn to make judgments about his choices. All books and stories are not equally good. All books and stories are not equally appreciated by all readers. Only by verbalizing his reactions can the reader determine the kinds of books or the particular books which are highly satisfactory to him. Tests for the good in literature can emerge only upon reflection of that which is not good. This series of questions enables the teacher to assess each reader's progress in the area of appreciation and tests.

Values gained from book. Questions of this sort are designed specifically to determine the extent to which the reader has responded in depth to the ideas in the book. All questions lead the reader into making a series of judgments about the worthwhileness of the ideas. Making such judgments about the relative importance of various ideas best defines the meaning of reading comprehension and is the best possible measure of it.

1. Did something happen in the book which you would like to have happen to you? Would you like to have been there and taken part in it?
2. Did something happen in the book which you would *not* like to have

happen to you? Reading about it was fun, but would you want to be there yourself?
3. Tell me a few highpoints of the book—some of the very best parts.
4. Which part of the book was most important? Why?
5. What do you think the person who wrote this book was trying to say to you?
6. Did this book tell or teach you something important that you did not know? or, What new ideas did you learn from reading this book?
7. How real (or imaginary) is this book?
8. Show how the writer made this book humorous (mysterious, adventurous, or life-like).

These questions cause the reader to make a judgment through selecting a part or parts of all ideas that have been read. The objective is to have the reader sort out ideas and order and arrange them in terms of their relative importance. It becomes reasonably easy for the teacher to tell whether the judgments made by the child are substantial or superficial. The teacher does not need to be intimately acquainted with all the books read by the children to discern the quality of the child's responses. The child reveals himself through his answers. The teacher knows immediately about the child's depth of understanding.

Obviously, only a few questions are asked of a particular child during any one conference. Time simply does not permit the use of many questions. Through the discussion of several books during a series of conferences over a period of time, almost all the questions will be employed on some occasion. In the actual conference situation, questions asked are often determined by the child's responses. Frequently a running repartee develops. One answer prompts another question. It should be clear, nevertheless, that the questions which have been presented are the kinds of questions asked. An effort is made to draw at least some questions from each of the three categories. The teacher's primary responsibility is to determine whether the child has exercised responsibility in his reading. A high degree of responsibility must accompany the freedom given to the child when he chooses books and reads them at his own rate.

A simulated dialogue between teacher and child follows.

The book: *The Sea Hunt** from the Under the Seas Series
The child: Age 9, Grade 3
T: "How did you find this book?"
P: "Oh, pretty good."
T: "What do you mean, pretty good?"

*Berres, Briscoe, Coleman, and Hewett, *The Sea Hunt*. San Francisco: Harr Wagner, 1959.

P: "Well, I liked it."
T: "Why did you like it?"
P: "It was exciting."
T: "What made it exciting?"
P: "A lot of things happened."
T: "Name one. Find the part where something exciting happened that you liked to read about but that you yourself wouldn't have wanted to experience. Can you find that part?"
P: "Yes." (P shows part where Carlos is pulled overboard by sharks, pp. 19-26.)
T: "Why was this the best part? What made it so good?"
P: "Because it was exciting. It was quite scary. I would have been afraid."
T: "What would you have done if you had been in Carlos' place?"
P: "I don't know. Carlos was right. He did the right thing when he splashed the water."
T: "Do you think you would have been as brave as Carlos?"
P: "Gee! I guess I would have to be. I'm not sure I would have been there in the first place."
T: "It's fun to read about it though. Will you read to me just the most scary part?"
P: (P reads two or three paragraphs on page 24. Oral reading is only fair, but more significantly P has shown ability to select important part.)
T: "That was good, wasn't it? Do you want to share this part of the book with the class?"
P: "Yes."
T: "All right! But be sure to practice so that you can do well when you read to the class. You will have to tell them how Carlos fell in and what made him fall in."
P: "I will."
T: "Of all the books which you have read, how does this one rate?"
P: "One of the best."
T: "Which books did you like better?"
P: *The Pearl Divers.**
T: "Why was that book better?"
P: "It was more exciting."
T: "Why? What made it more exciting?"
P: "The fight with the Devil Shark."
T: "Was this book hard or easy?"

*Berres, Briscoe, Coleman, and Hewett, *The Pearl Divers*. San Francisco: Harr Wagner, 1959.

P: "Easy. I knew all the words. It was easier than *The Pearl Divers*."
T: "Did you understand all that you read?"
P: "Yes."
T: "Did you get mixed up any place?"
P: "Only once, but I went back over it and I was O.K."
T: "Good! Did you learn some important new things?"
P: "Yes. A lot about the sea."
T: "That's good. You may go back to your seat. You already have your next book, don't you?"
P: "Yes."

The example reveals that questions flow from answers given by the students. The best questions must truly be the result of the teacher's knowledge of the child and the book which he is reading. The mood of the moment created by this interaction of the teacher, the child, and *his* book provides the stimulation to evoke the best questions. By utilizing this approach, deep insight is gained into both the child and the quality of his reading. As a consequence, the individual conference is the high point of evaluation for both child and teacher.

The Diagnostic Teacher-Pupil Conference

All individual conferences are diagnostic in the sense that continuous observations are being made about the individual child, his books, and his approach to reading them. There are, however, some highly specialized activities and particular points of inquiry which can be used to pinpoint unusual difficulties which frequently confront some children. Again, in this second model a typical set of observations and questions is presented to provide a framework within which the teacher can work.

Major Concern: An Observation Must Be Made Regarding Difference Between the Level of Word Recognition and the Level of Understanding

It is essential to notice the extent of the difference between the child's power with oral language and his power with printed language. Assessing the child's power with oral language comes from a variety of prior situations: his oral contributions, his responses to oral examinations, and his spontaneous remarks during informal conversations. If the performance in oral language is markedly higher than in printed language, the problem area lies largely in the word recognition area rather than in the thought-response area.

A. Key Question on Sight Recognition and Understanding

If the ability to recognize words were markedly increased, would the ability to understand ideas in printed material remain much the same, be somewhat improved, or be greatly improved?

The above question pinpoints the observation. If the child were granted power of word recognition equal to that possessed by the typical child in the class, would his power of understanding the printed word be drastically improved? A pivotal choice point lies in the answer to this question. If "yes," the child's skill in word recognition must be carefully analyzed. If "no," the child's ability to think when words serve as the vehicle for such thought must be further examined. Examination of word recognition skills, though carried out, would be of lesser importance.

The procedure for thoroughly investigating sight word recognition and related word skills will be presented first.

B. *The First Alternative: Skills in Reading*
  1. Key Question on Sufficiency of Sight Recognition Vocabulary: Does the child have the necessary sight word recognition skills and how well does he use these skills? More precisely, at what point does the child's response to the unique appearance of the total word form break down?

     Observe through Pointing to Words test. Proceed by asking the child to respond instantly to the word shown. Point to words in the book; begin with easy common words and work up through difficult, common to uncommon, and finally easy to difficult complex words. Start from the bottom of any page and work up the page (s) by pointing to words until the kinds of words no longer recognized by sight are evident. The material which the child is reading at the time is suitable for this test.

  2. Key Question on Word Study Skills: What word analysis skills are typically employed when the child no longer responds to uniqueness of total word form?

     Observe by asking the child to tell you what approach he is using as he is studying words. Tell him to "Do it out loud so I can hear what you are doing." Record the appropriate responses.
     a. The child studies the word visually by looking carefully at the word form. The typical response is, "I am just staring it down" (like Davey Crockett's bear).
     b. The child determines the word from the contextual setting. The typical response is, "I read the other words around it; it fits."
     c. The child removes beginnings or endings to see familiar parts. The typical response to the unknown word *factual* is, "I covered up the ending (*ual*) and put (*f*) with *act*. I can get *fact* but I can't get the end (*ual*)."

d. The child discerns the relationship which exists among words. The typical response to the unknown word (*spent*) is, "I took the *sp* off and tried *t*; I got *tent* so I put the *sp* back and got *spent*."
e. The child sounds isolated letters in turn while attempting to make the total word emerge. The typical response to the unknown word *break* is a murmured "ber ē kuh . . . brēek." T: "Have you heard brēek; is it a word?" P: "No!" T: "When the baseball hits the window, what happens?"
f. The child divides words into syllables. The typical response to the unknown word *conversational* is, "Cŏn-ver-săt′ . . . No! Cŏn vĕr sā′ tion al."

Through repeated separate observation periods during conference time, the teacher can build a picture of each child's approach to word study. Each child's characteristic pattern can be recorded through the following check form.

Characteristic Word Study Patterns

  i. Impetuous Approach—Guesses wildly
     Generalizations cause errors by child's saying
       only one letter or word part (*rurv* for *river*)
       only first letter (*boy* for *big*)
       only similar ending (*and* for *said*)
       word in reverse (*was* for *saw*)
  ii. Taciturn Approach—waits and does nothing
  iii. Friendly Puppy Approach—looks to you for help
  iv. Fugitive Approach—appears nervous and glances about (does not look at book)
      Utters series of *ah's* and *uh's* to gain time
  v. Tenacious Approach—persists in efforts, brushes away help, initial response incorrect but frequently corrects self quickly

Through teacher observation, decisions are made regarding the placement of the child in a skills development group. In addition, the teacher determines skill areas which need to be taught through systematic instruction to various skills groups.

3. Key Question on Levels of Silent Reading Efficiency: What level(s) of efficiency does the child exhibit during Uninterrupted Sustained Silent Reading (USSR)? Basic proficiency levels to be observed follow:

   a. Look-Say (L-S) is the lowest efficiency level. It is characterized by the child's saying each word to himself and is equivalent to oral reading-with-the-volume-turned-down. Slow, laborious silent read-

ing ensues and signifies too much attention to word study and too little to thought-getting response.
   b. Look-Hear (L-H) is a low efficiency level. It is characterized by some observable vocalization but mainly by slowness in accomplishing coverage of material. The child answers affirmatively to the question, When reading to yourself do you seem to hear someone saying most of the words to you?
   c. Look-Think$_1$ (L-Th$_1$) is a higher efficiency level. It is characterized by the use of a look-think response process. However, because of looking at each and every word, effort to reconstruct the unfolding pattern of ideas is only partially successful.
   d. Look-Think$_2$ (L-Th$_2$) is the highest efficiency level. It is characterized by efficient thought-getting process. Child, by scanning lines, seizes on those words powerpacked with meaning and, thereby, reconstructs and orders important ideas rapidly.

In classrooms where teachers stress silent reading (such as occurs in the Individualized Reading Program) many opportunities exist to observe silent reading efficiency levels maintained by pupils. Where the teacher values uninterrupted sustained silent reading (USSR) as the acme of all skill development activity, observations should be made frequently and carefully. As pupils gain proficiency, they will spend longer periods with sustained concentration on silent reading. Logging time spent, by keeping a daily record of USSR, over several months of time is a valuable adjunct to the total evaluation activity.

During the diagnostic conference time, the teacher reviews progress the pupil is making in sustaining himself in ever increasing lengths of time during the silent reading. As the conference proceeds, she may designate a particular passage to be read silently. While the child reads, the teacher makes a particular effort to observe efficiency levels utilized by the pupil. To test for flexibility, the pupil is asked to find quickly the words which answer specific questions—questions so posed that answers lie scattered throughout the material. Thus the child must use L-Th$_2$ to complete the task correctly. The extent to which the child is able or unable to do so reveals the relative inefficiency or efficiency level of silent reading. Generally this observational test is carried out with material the child is currently reading. Helpful hints for improving silent reading skills will be presented in the subsequent section on the total class conference.

C. The Second Alternative: Thinking with the Printed Word

Some children have power in word recognition and related skills but flounder when asked to respond meaningfully to the printed word. They simply do not think well with printed words. This model or type, while not so apparent as the non-word recognizer, can be readily detected through the more general teacher-pupil conference and the questions typically asked therein. But there are several specific observational activities and inquiries which sharpen the focus in examining the problem. Teachers can and should learn to use them.

1. Key Question on Meaningful Response Uninterrupted Sustained Silent Reading (USSR): In USSR is the child's response essentially and consistently a meaningful experience?

    The teacher must observe basically the extent to which the child sorts and orders ideas in terms of their relative importance. To test this, both short and longer selections (some pre-read and some not pre-read) should be used. A quick check test can readily be devised from the book or material the child is currently reading. The check test should be at three levels of complexity—the word level, the sentence level, and the paragraph level. In the last instance a series of paragraphs is frequently used.

2. Key Question on Words and Phrases: Can the child mentally translate word meanings and show proper use of abstract word or phrase units?

    To test this ability, select four or five of the more difficult or unusual words or word phrases on pages close to where the child is reading. Ask for an interpretation of meaning. To be more exacting ask the child to read the sentence containing a word or idiomatic expression, but have him substitute an appropriate word or words for the difficult ones in question. "Read this sentence to me; put in a word or words for *concoction*, but keep the meaning nearly the same." Sample sentence: He stirred the funny colored *concoction*. P: "Would *mixture* fit?" T: "Yes, I think so."

3. Key Question on Selecting Ideas: Can the child select important ideas from a paragraph? Observational test: Select a paragraph and skim it. Tell the child to find the sentence or sentences which tell him most about the paragraph. Persist in pinpointing exact words and phrases which are most powerpacked with meaning. "Show me the place where it tells you that . . . ." "Which word or words in the sentence are of greatest importance?"

The questions enumerated previously under "Values Gained From Book" should reveal how the child manages longer selections wherein ideas are interwoven into complex and intricate patterns. The child's ability to handle the unfolding of ideas is the ultimate test of proficient reading.

Observations pertaining to attitudes toward, commitments to, and involvement in reading books can be gained by utilizing questions previously suggested under the heading of "Appreciation of Book." The topic of appraising oral reading has been treated extensively in the literature on informal reading inventories. The title of an IRA Reading Aids Booklet by the same name is fairly definitive; thus, the evaluation of oral reading skills has not been included in this paper (2).

The Small Group Conference

A seldom used but highly effective teaching procedure is to call a group of youngsters to the reading circle according to kinds of books being read. "Anyone who is reading a mystery story please bring your book to the reading table." *Mystery story* can be replaced by *funny story, fantasy story, adventure story, biography, science story, animal story,* etc.

The ensuing discussion is based upon the thematic characteristic represented among the books brought to the group situation by the children. A discussion of books characterized as fanciful or imaginative might unfold in the following manner.

Teacher: "Each of you has a book which is imaginative, haven't you? Some of the books are really fantastic, like Jean's Dr. Seuss book. David, is your book more like reporting—telling what happened and how it happened—or is it quite imaginative?"

David: "Boy, it's wild!"

(Several other children are queried concerning the relative factual to highly imaginative dimension. The books vary with regard to this quality; the teacher emphasizes the reality-fantasy continuum.)

Teacher: "How do we get books which are fanciful? Where do these ideas come from?"

Debbie: "From the author."

Teacher: "Yes, but where does the writer get these ideas?"

Ken: "In his head."

Teacher: "Yes, in his mind; he makes them up. Can we say that these books are really true; do the things in them really take place?"

Children: "No!"

Anne: "Most of the things in my book couldn't happen."

Teacher: "Can we say these ideas are real ideas?"

Albert: "Ya! Some guy thought 'em up. He had 'em in his head. He got them from somewhere."

Teacher: "But there is a difference between telling what actually happened and telling about something we just imagine happened."

Children in Chorus: "Yes."

Robin: "But they sure make some wonderful reading."

Teacher: "Now I want each of you to find in your book one or two places where the ideas are most fantastic, where the writer has told something that just couldn't happen. We'll see who has a part in his book with the most imagination."

(The children search for places in their books exemplifying the greatest degrees of fantasy. Turns are given to various children to read the fanciful parts; following several renditions according to limits of time, a decision is made regarding the greatest display of imagination by the various authors. Two or three children steadfastly maintain that their particular book is most fanciful.)

This abbreviated and to some extent simulated discussion is intended to show how fundamental qualities basic to reading comprehension can be developed through group discussion. The teacher, by observing reactions of various children, can add to her catalogue of items about each child's reading. Does the child respond to the finer discriminations within the dimension of reality—fantasy? A teacher must observe these responses to truly know the child as a reader. It is vital to the total evaluation process.

Similar dialogues could have been presented for a variety of qualities found between the covers but below the surface print of hundreds of children's books. Several more important qualities follow:

Humor — extend understanding of what constitutes funniness and humor.

Biography — fidelity with which the qualities and characteristics of the central person are developed. (Is there an honest portrayal of positive and negative elements?)

Mystery — manner by which the writer developed the aura of mystery and the extent to which situations are contrived or natural.

Family Situation — exploration of validity with which the author recorded behavior and reactions of persons within the story to critical choice points. (How would the children who are reading react in similar conflicting situations?)

The combined responses given by children over a series of group conferences become highly revealing. The generalized impressions the teacher gains about a particular child can be refined and verified within the scope of the individual teacher-pupil conference. Thus, the group conference is a valuable part of the total evaluation program.

The Total Class Conference Following Silent Reading Time

Through the personal conference the teacher really learns about each child as a reader and about the books he chooses to read. The richness of the personal contact makes the conference uniquely vital. There is so much to talk about, so many books; there is always the desire to prolong the conference. But always there are so many children. Of course, there is not enough time to talk sufficiently with each child. Many truly interesting conferences have to be cut short.

Teachers often ask, Where does one find time—any time—for individual conferences? Gaining time for a personal conference with each child is possible only if the proper atmosphere prevails during the reading period. The concept of a *silent reading time* or a *quiet reading time* is basic. To establish this setting the teacher must hold strong, positive convictions about the value of Uninterrupted Sustained Silent Reading (USSR). Effort, energy, and determination must be given to the establishment of a reading time wherein sustained silent reading is continually being developed and expanded. Progressing as a reader requires the child to pace himself with increased amounts of silent reading time.

To augment suggestions presented under the heading "Levels of Silent Reading Efficiency," a brief evaluation period can be held with the total class at the conclusion of the daily USSR. Again the artistry of teaching is exhibited through the questions asked. Several suggested questions are listed which can be used effectively to prime the discussion. The teacher must realize that on any given day a different combination of questions could be used.

1. Did you have a good reading period today? Did you read well?
2. Did you read better today than yesterday?
3. Were you able to concentrate today on your silent reading?
4. Did the ideas in the book hold your attention?
5. Did you have the feeling of wanting to go ahead faster to find out what happened? Were you constantly moving ahead with the ideas?
6. Was it hard for you to keep your mind on what you were reading today?
7. Were you bothered by others or by outside noises?
8. Could you keep the ideas in your book straight in your mind?
9. Did you get mixed up in any place? Did you have to go back and straighten yourself out?
10. Were there words you did not know? How did you figure them out?
11. What did you do when you got to the good parts? Did you read faster or slower?

By generating a discussion about the nature, quality, and quantity of reading accomplished by the class during USSR, the teacher helps to build a concept within each child about the kind of reader he is becoming and of what he needs to do to improve. This evaluation session, while brief, can be invaluable. The child is able to see the kind of reader he needs to be. The result is evaluation in the best sense of the word.

Summary

By proclamation, personal evaluation through teacher-pupil conferences has been declared superior to all other approaches to pupil evaluation. It has not been claimed to be the easiest; undoubtedly, it is the most difficult, but the effort must be made. Certainly, evaluation is much more than the stone-cold scores recorded on the class roster for the achievement test given last month. It is more than the nebulous number which supposedly represents a certain grade level performance derived from an informal reading inventory. (The figure 3.2 may have significance for beverages, but what does it really tell us about a child's reading?)

Getting the right answers about each child's reading hinges on asking the right questions. Every teacher, fortified with the proper array of questions and oriented to perceptive observations, can be and must be the central figure in the total evaluation process. Only the teacher is in a position to know the child as a reader and to recognize the impact which books have upon him. After all, this is what reading is all about.

REFERENCES

1. Hunt, Lyman. *The Key to the Conference Lies in the Questioning*.
2. Kress, Roy, and Marjorie Johnson. *Informal Reading Inventories*. Newark, Delaware: International Reading Association, 1965.
3. Sandberg, Herbert H. (Ed.). *Educational Comment on Individual Reading*. Toledo, Ohio: University of Toledo, 1966.

DAVID W. DARLING
INTERAMERICAN EDUCATIONAL CENTER
SAN ANTONIO, TEXAS

10. Evaluating the Affective Dimension of Reading

Two major topics are considered in this paper. First, there is a discussion of ways in which a teacher of reading can teach for and evaluate affective behavior in reading. This discussion is intended to set the stage for the second section of the paper which is a description and an analysis of Krathwohl's (2) *Taxonomy of Educational Objectives for the Affective Domain* and its role in the evaluation of affective reading behaviors.

Teaching Behavior and the Affective Dimension of Reading

Begin by looking into the act of teaching and analyzing it in terms of affective evaluation in reading. What are some of the things teachers do that influence what children learn?
- Teachers ask questions and make comments.
- They respond to students' questions, ideas, and actions.
- They explain and make assignments.
- They prepare and give tests.
- They record and issue grades.
- Teachers project an image.

Other behaviors could be included, but those listed above can be used as a basis for the present discussion.

Before moving into the discussion of teacher behavior, think of a "good" reading group you have had. Think of individuals within the group. Who was anxious to approach the reading "circle"? Which member of the group would rather participate in reading than in most other school activities? Who tended to act like some of the characters in the stories that were read? Who was eager to respond to questions and to other pupils' comments? As these questions concerning the reading group and individuals in the group are answered, the affective behavior of the students is being evaluated and an attempt is being made to get an understanding of the group's *feeling* about reading. Those who are most eager for reading instruction, those who let the content of what they read affect what they do, are operating at very high levels of affective behavior.

Now picture in the mind's eye a "poor" reading group. Who in this group shows a clear willingness to respond to questions? Who shows no initiative in responding but will answer if called upon? Who would let his attention wander while in the circle? Who will seldom respond to questions but is willing to pay attention to what is being said. Again, as these questions are answered the learner's affective behavior is being evaluated. A learner who is willing to attend but not willing to respond is operating at a very low level of affective behavior. He does not feel very good about reading; he is not emotionally committed to reading. These are important considerations for teachers as they analyze their pupils' progress. Reading teachers may make this kind of informal evaluation of each child frequently and adjust teaching strategies accordingly.

Each time a teacher asks a question, receives a response, and indicates a feeling about that response, he has engaged in a form of evaluation. This is a very important evaluation because these frequent teacher-pupil transactions are strong conditioners of what a child learns about reading and how he feels about it. Too often, evaluation is only thought of in terms of the six-weeks test, the annual achievement tests, or other written tests.

Now, look at each of the teaching behaviors mentioned previously. The first such behavior is teacher questioning during a reading lesson. One good source of questions is the teachers' edition of a basal reader. Following are some examples of questions selected randomly from what are considered to be "good" reading series.

These questions are suggested in a teacher's edition for a story about Charlie Brave, an Indian boy who had lived in the city until his recent move to the reservation, and the trouble he experienced with interpersonal relations. In the first set of questions the answer can be found in or inferred from the text.

- Why was it hard for Charlie to make friends with the boys on the reservation?
- In what way did Charlie think his sister was more fortunate than he?
- What happened that gave Charlie another chance to try to make friends?
- Why do you suppose no one on the reservation had been willing to try goat's milk before?

The next two questions are a little different. They offer the opportunity for the learner to read himself into the story.

- Do you think Charlie and the boys learned something about one another?

- Do you think Charlie's life on the reservation will be different or much the same from now on? Why? (2)

The first set of questions asked for a cognitive response. The teacher, having read the story, knows which answers to accept as correct and which to reject as incorrect. In the second set of questions, only the responder knows the answer. If the teacher accepts any answer the responder gives, perhaps following with questions to help the pupil clarify his position, the question is in the affective domain. The learner is asked to respond in reference to his own value base, hence the student is reading his own feelings and emotions into Charlie's behavior. However, if the teacher has a preconceived answer which he expects, and pursues the questions until he gets his desired answer or seeks consensus among the students, the question becomes a cognitive one. Responses which the reader is supposed to deduce logically from the behavior displayed in the story, or which can be derived by accepting an outside value system, are cognitive replies.

This distinction is seldom made clear to teachers in the teacher's edition. As a result, most affective questions in texts are treated by teachers as cognitive ones. The affective questions that do appear in texts are often lost. Or worse, perhaps the pupil is conditioned not to read himself into the story and thereby loses the tremendous benefits of personal involvement in reading. Or he may be conditioned to accept a value system that is not his own.

Here is another set of questions intended to train the learner in forming judgments about events in a story. The story is about a chimpanzee named Josephine who was found in a jungle, raised in a private home, and finally turned over to a zoo. Which questions can legitimately be answered only by reference to the responder's feelings and emotions?

- Why do you think Josephine was afraid in the jungle?
- Why do you think the man took Josephine home?
- Why do you think people were always saying, No, no, to Josephine?
- Why do you think the keeper let Josephine into the hall?
- Why did Josephine lick the pan and the cloth?
- What would you do if Josephine were your pet? Why? (6)

The first, third, and fifth questions likely are *not* affective questions for there are either subtle or direct clues in the story which can be used as a referent for responding. The second, fourth, and sixth may evoke affective responses since no clue to the answer is given in the context of the story.

The last questions were selected to illustrate that it is difficult to determine whether a question asks for cognitive or affective behavior unless one knows the context of the story. Thus, there are two simple criteria that can be applied by teachers either to frame affective questions or to recognize affective questions appearing in teachers' editions: (a) the answer cannot be inferred easily from the story, and (b) the responder is the sole determiner of the validity of the response. These are affective questions because they require the responder to become more personally involved in the story. They ask him to apply his values, feelings, or emotions to the situations presented, not merely to recall that which is explicitly stated or may be logically inferred from the story.

The vast majority of questions and comments appearing in teachers' editions are in the cognitive realm. These questions are designed to teach the pupil such word attack skills as structural analysis, phonetic analysis, contextual analysis, comprehension and interpretation skills, study skills, and the like—all cognitive skills. They deal with what a child knows, what he can recall, and what he can interpret or infer from what he knows.

Affective questions seldom appear in the texts, although they are more frequently found in reading than in other types of texts. They are normally found in sections which are designed to teach comprehension, interpretation, or creative reading.

If one feels it is important for the learner to attach positive worth to becoming personally involved in reading, then one must ask those questions which will bring forth and reward such behavior. Questions requesting affective responses must be asked. The responses to such questions must be respected and acknowledged. The whole climate should be set to encourage the learner to become personally involved in reading.

To this point the discussion has centered on evaluating affective behavior by using questions in teachers' editions. Certainly teachers ask many questions that do not appear in the manuals. (I have not made an extensive study of teacher-student interaction situations but recall from my frequent observations of instruction that affective questions are seldom asked during reading instruction. For this paper I analyzed samples of teacher-student interactions from two second, two fourth, and two sixth grade reading classes. I am indebted to Dr. Frank J. Guszak for these examples (*1*).

In these classroom episodes, the six teachers asked a total of about 260 questions. Of these 260 questions, none were in the affective domain. All 260 questions asked for, and received, cognitive responses. The void in rewarding affective behavior in the day-to-day classroom conditioning process is dramatically clear. The reader is supposed to *know* what he has read. Whether the reader has any feelings about the stories or whether he has personally involved himself in the reading is apparently immaterial, for these teachers made no effort to determine this aspect. Stated differently, if teachers desired the learners to achieve any affective objectives, they would have had to ask questions which would elicit an affective response.

Since no such questions were asked, one must assume that the teachers had no such objectives. Few people would admit that they are not vitally concerned about children developing a love of reading. Love is an affective behavior, not a cognitive one. Naturally, one cannot generalize from a population of only six teachers, but the interactions appearing in Guszak's dissertation do not differ from what one normally sees occurring in classrooms.

Some of the teacher-student exchanges did solicit affective behavior. A few short episodes follow for examination.

T: Now, John looked surprised. Why?
S: Because he didn't know he (his friend) was going to say that.
T: Well, what else?
S: He didn't know he was going to the park—that big park.
T: Yes, he thought what?

The first question may be open for the reader to analyze the "surprise" feeling in terms of his own behavior, which is probably what the first child does. The reader was probably himself surprised when "he said that." But the teacher wanted a specific cognitive response from the story and disregarded the child's response by saying, "Well, what else?" The teacher might have responded with "Is that where you were surprised?" or "When would you have been surprised?" When the teacher received the answer she wanted (he found he was going to the big park), she responded with "Yes, he thought what?" thus affirming the cognitive response she was seeking.

Here is another short sequence taken from a sixth grade lesson.

T: What gave Giuseppe pleasure, Eddie? Where did he get the most pleasure?
S: When the man fixed the organ.
T: Jackie, what do you think gave him the most pleasure?
S: Composing.
T: Isn't that what he likes best of all? He liked music best.

You can see that it is difficult to select passages which might lend themselves to affective questioning. The interchange is clearly a cognitive one. However, the first response may have been an affective reply. The pupil may have been describing the event in the story which gave him pleasure. The teacher failed to sense this fact and pursued the question until she acquired the acceptable answer. Thus, in effect, she discouraged the pupil from becoming personally involved in the story. Very few of the other 260 questions asked by these teachers came even this close to evoking an affective response.

The second type of teaching behavior that determines what a child learns is the teacher's responding to things pupils say and do. Students look upon this function as a real form of evaluation. Teachers must become aware and take advantage of these constant opportunities for evaluation and clarification. Raths, Harmin, and Simon (4) have an excellent treatment of such a teaching strategy in their book *Values and Teaching*. The book contains, among other things, a detailed responding technique which teachers can use to help learners clarify their own values.

> The responding strategy is a way of responding to a student that results in his considering what he has chosen, what he prizes, and/or what he is doing. It stimulates him to clarify his thinking and behavior and thus to clarify his values; it encourages him to think about them.

The authors list and discuss ten elements which are essential if the teacher is to help learners clarify their values.

> 1. The clarifying response avoids moralizing, criticizing, giving values, or evaluating. The adult excludes all hints of "good" or "right" or "acceptable," or their opposites, in such responses.
> 2. It puts the responsibility on the student to look at his behavior or his ideas and to think and decide for himself what it is he wants.
> 3. A clarifying response also entertains the possibility that the student will *not* look or decide or think. It is permissive and stimulating but not insistent.
> 4. It does not try to do big things with its small comments. It works more at stimulating thought relative to what a person does or says. It aims at setting a mood. Each clarifying response is only one of many; the effect is cumulative.
> 5. Clarifying responses are not used for interview purposes. The goal is not to obtain data but for the student to clarify his ideas and life if he wants to do so.
> 6. It is usually not an extended discussion. The idea is for the student to think, and he usually does that best alone, without the temptation to justify his thoughts to an adult. Therefore, a teacher will be advised to carry on only two or three rounds of dialogue and then offer to break off the conversation with some noncommittal but honest phrase.
> 7. Clarifying responses are often for individuals. A topic in which John might need clarification may be of no immediate interest to Mary.
> 8. The teacher doesn't respond to everything everyone says or does in a classroom. There are other responsibilities he has.
> 9. Clarifying responses operate in situations in which there are no "right" answers, such as in situations involving feelings, attitudes, beliefs, or purposes. They are *not* appropriate for drawing a student toward a predetermined answer.
> 10. Clarifying responses are not mechanical things that carefully follow a formula. They must be used creatively and with insight, but with their purpose in mind (4).

These ten conditions are not simple to bring about since they require conscious effort and practice on the part of teachers if the strategy is to be successfully implemented. One brief example will give some understanding of this approach.

S: I felt sad when I finished the story.
T: Were you glad you felt that way?
S: Well, sort of—I mean, the story was very interesting and I liked it even if it did have a sad ending.
T: Would you read this kind of story again?
S: Well, maybe—especially if I didn't mind feeling sad, I would.
T: I see. Mary, what story did you read? (Switching to another student.)

A few of the major characteristics of this technique are (a) the transactions are very short, usually only two or three exchanges; (b) the teacher's questions require the student to reflect on his own feelings, attitudes, or behavior; and (c) the sequence is terminated with a non-committal statement by the teacher with the learner being neither rewarded nor punished.

This is a process of helping pupils to value rather than of teaching any special set of values. The method sounds simple, but it is not. To acquire competency in helping learners to clarify their own feelings or values requires diligent practice by the teacher. It is also difficult to plan for since it is used advantageously only in response to what students do or say at any time. Teachers need to become sensitive to situations involving feelings, attitudes, purposes, or beliefs, and be able to *ad lib* appropriate clarifying responses. Raths' book is an immensely valuable tool for this purpose.

The clarifying response strategy shifts the burden of evaluation from the teacher to the student. The teacher asks questions which help the student become aware of additional information or attitudes and leaves it to the student to think through the situation and make judgments. This is a legitimate form of evaluation which is quite consistent with the goal of helping learners develop tools for self discipline. The shift from evaluation by the teacher to evaluation by the learner is an important change. When the teacher ceases to be the distributor of rewards and punishments he, in effect, ceases to be the evaluator. The teacher's clarifying responses do not give the student any clues about how the teacher feels. The learner is left dangling and must form his own judgments about the worth of his feelings and actions.

The third thing that teachers do is to give explanations and assignments. These are only indirectly related to evaluation. The point to be made here is that explanations and assignments need to reflect the teacher's concern for the affective development of the learners and should be, in part, an outgrowth of previous assessment and evaluation of the student's attitudes toward reading and what he reads.

The fourth teaching behavior, the preparation and administration of tests, is an important evaluation practice. To judge teachers' attempts to evaluate affective behavior in reading, a small sample of teacher-made tests were collected from reading teachers who were acknowledged as "good."

In these examinations, a total of about 350 questions or statements required the student to make a response. Only two questions offered the slightest possibility for a child to contribute an affective response; the rest clearly called for some kind of cognitive behavior. The two examples follow:
- How do you think the boys felt when they heard the howling noise?
- Be a god or godess (*sic*) and tell what good thing you would do to help or change something in the world.

These are both weak. The first could perhaps be and probably was answered from the context of the story. The second has an aura of morality and unrealness to it.

What about the other 348 queries? For the most part they were good questions calling for a good range of *cognitive* behavior.

The sample used in this analysis was too small to permit one to generalize with confidence; however, it is strongly doubtful that a more extensive study would change the results significantly. The tests written by these teachers were consistent in the kinds of questions asked when compared to the oral questions reported in the Guszak study (*1*).

What about grading affective reading behavior? This is the fifth type of teacher behavior. Currently, only cognitive behaviors are graded—for example, the basic reading skills and reading comprehension. A learner's interests, values, and beliefs in relation to reading are not graded. It is quite likely that the reason teachers do not ask valuing questions either orally or on tests is because valuing is not graded. There is an almost overwhelming tendency to teach only those things one is going to grade. It is also common for a pupil to learn those things upon which he is going to be graded. Teachers seem to be saying, "Why waste time on something that isn't reported on?" Pupils reflect this same feeling. It is unlikely that affective behavior will be evaluated by the great majority of teachers unless the very practical task of grading and reporting a pupil's affective growth is undertaken. A grade is an indicator of a learner's progress and, as such, is a record or a reporting of an evaluative judgment. The grade, as a product of evaluation, is less a conditioner of behavior than are the constant interactions described earlier. However, a teacher may look to what is going to be graded to find clues to aid in determining the conditioning strategies he will employ. This basic issue extends beyond the scope of this paper.

Finally, the teacher projects a total image. If a teacher is committed to helping children come to cherish reading, it will be evident to her pupils. If a teacher is committed to teaching her pupils to read, even if it kills them, this attitude will come through. The constant din of the teaching of phonetics, syllabication, interpretation, comprehension, and the like stresses the importance of cognitive skills. Of course, one could not become committed to reading without mastery of the basic skills; but one can master all these skills and still not enjoy reading, be committed to reading, nor use reading for the purpose for which it is presumably taught—to enrich one's life. Some learners will come to enjoy reading regardless of what teachers do. But the goal is and must be to have all pupils become committed to reading—a goal requiring conscious effort.

The Affective Domain

Thanks to extensive research, quite a lot about teaching the cognitive reading skills is known. Due to the lack of extensive research, very little about teaching for affective behavior in reading is available. It appears that we have fallen into the trap of which John Mann recently warned; we are putting all our energy into that about which we know the most at the expense of that about which we care the most (*3*).

Four things must be done to correct this deficiency: (a) teachers' editions and manuals of reading textbooks must put greater emphasis on affective questions and testing; (b) extensive research must be carried out to bring about a balance in what we know about both the affective and cognitive aspects of reading; (c) pupils' affective growth in reading must be tested and reported; and (d) teacher education programs should be expanded so that those entering teaching will have competence in teaching the basic skills and in guiding the learner's affective development.

The acceptance of a general taxonomy of affective behavior or one specifically for reading would be a distinct asset in accomplishing these four tasks. To analyze its applicability, it would be interesting to use the Krathwohl Taxonomy as a basis for affective evaluation in reading (*2*).

An attempt has been made to use the term *affective* in the same sense it is used in Krathwohl's handbook. Affective behavior emphasizes a feeling tone, an emotion, or a degree of acceptance or rejection. Learning activities which are aimed at developing interests, attitudes, values, and appreciation are all in the affective realm.

It may be recalled that there are five levels in the hierarchical continuum of the affective taxonomy: (a) *Receiving*, (b) *Responding*, (c) *Valuing*, (d) *Organizing*, and (e) *Characterization*. The continuum extends from a simple *awareness* on one extreme to *complete internalization* on the other.

One way to view the taxonomy is in terms of personal involvement. If a learner is sporadic in his attentiveness during reading, if he is *receiving* sometimes—but not all the time—then his degree of personal involvement is very low. On the other hand, if he is an avid reader and seeks to immerse himself in reading, then he is committed to reading and is personally involved to a high degree. The taxonomy represents a continuum of varying degrees of personal involvement.

Another way to look at the taxonomy is in terms of internalization. This is the organizing thread Krathwohl and others have accepted (2). Internalization describes the process by which the act of reading may progressively become an integral part of the individual.

Reading can be valued for itself or it can be used to study and evaluate the other parts of one's total value system. Thus, one can learn to value reading itself and one can be committed to utilizing reading to build a consistent value system. Both are legitimate objectives of education and both should be evaluated.

In the Receiving category, three levels of behavior have been identified: (a) *awareness*, (b) *willingness to receive*, and (c) *controlled attention*. These are close to being cognitive behaviors. It is not generally necessary to test or ask questions to ascertain learner behavior at this level. The day dreamer, the sporadic listener, the one who is occasionally with you and occasionally not—each is on this level. These persons show a lack of interest *as well as* skills. The teacher can usually spot these by consciously reflecting on each child and his overt behavior during reading instruction.

Three levels of behavior have been identified in the Responding category: (a) *acquiescence in responding*, (b) *willingness to respond*, and (c) *satisfaction in response*.

These behaviors are most evident when the learner has an opportunity to respond during reading instruction. A teacher can check this fact occasionally by keeping a small chart to tally pupils' responses. Each time Sally must be requested to answer, a tally goes in the *acquiescence in responding* box. When she volunteers a response but indicates no strong feeling about having responded, a tally goes in the *willingness to respond* category. If Sally volunteers a reply and indicates she feels good or happy about having answered, the mark goes in the *satisfaction in response* box. A total of tallies in each box will render a rough indication of the child's responding level. This informal evaluation is simple and will help focus the teacher's attention on affective behavior. Evaluating responding behavior should be of major importance to teachers, and informal assessment should be made periodically.

The three levels of Valuing behavior, (a) *acceptance of a value*, (b) *preference for a value*, and (c) *commitment to a value*, are rather high levels of affective behavior. These usually develop over a longer period of time.

Elementary teachers often use charts to record books pupils have read and to give an added incentive for pupils to read trade books. These teachers are attempting to get the students *to accept the value* of reading. Billy reads more trade books so he can be ahead of Mary on the chart. In the process, he finds that there is satisfaction to be gained from reading. Later, hopefully, when the stimulus chart is removed, the pupil will continue to prefer reading to some other activities. At this point, it can be said that if the learner likes to read, he is *accepting the value* of reading.

To determine whether a student has acquired a *preference for reading*, he needs to be given the opportunity to make a choice. Many teachers have a reading table, an activity table, and the like in their rooms. If Susan has the choice of reading a book, working a puzzle, or writing a story, and if she chooses reading, it could be said that Susan is operating at the second level of valuing. She has developed a *preference for reading*, at least over the stipulated alternatives. Keeping a record of the free time choices made by students could give another indication of the student's affective development in reading.

This category also lends itself to paper and pencil testing. Reading preference inventories could be used, or it would not be difficult to find personal preference inventories that could be adapted for assessment in this area.

Developing a *commitment for reading* is a high and noble aspiration. This is the highest level of Valuing behavior. It is usually not difficult to determine when a pupil is committed to reading. When he has a free moment, he is reading. Reading is *very* high on his list of preferred activities. He has a tendency to channel his reading in a special area and shifts to a new area only after he has probed deeply into his current interest. A teacher can evaluate a commitment by observation, much the same as she can evaluate Receiving behavior by observation. The teacher should look for (a) constant reading, (b) depth reading in special areas, and (c) a dependence on reading as a means of recreation as well as a means of becoming informed.

A person that has become committed to reading may use reading as a means of exploring and further refining his whole value system. That is, a reader committed to reading may use reading *for* developing, ordering, and structuring a comprehensive, consistent value system that becomes his person.

Rath's (4) clarifying response strategies assess behavior and require the learner to operate at the three highest levels of the affective taxonomy—Valuing, which we have just been discussing; Organizing; and Characterization. This contention is consistent with the idea that the Taxonomy is a continuum of progressive internalization. External measures and standards may be used to evaluate the first three levels: Receiving, Responding, and Valuing. Internal measures and standards may be used to evaluate at the three highest levels: Valuing, Organizing, and Characterization. Notice that Valuing is the transitional link on the internalization continuum where both external and internal evaluation may take place.

The major referent used here for evaluating at these three higher levels is essentially Rath's clarifying response strategy. The substance being evaluated shifts generally from reading as a behavior to the material one has read. The technique uses the content of what one has read to help him recognize commitments, help him conceptualize what he values, and aid him in organizing his value system.

Returning to the second Valuing level, *preference for a value*, teachers' questions such as "What is good about this book (or story)?" or "What books did you reject before you settled on your present selection?" are asking the learner to clarify his preference for a value. The first question asks the learner to reflect on what is "good" about his choice, while the latter asks him to relate his choice to discarded choices.*

A teacher is asking the reader to test his *commitment to a value* when he asks such questions as "Are you willing to recommend that author to the class?" or "Would you be willing to write a paper supporting the author's point of view?" These questions tend to test the student's commitment by asking him to reflect on the extent to which he is willing to make his own views and values public information and to take action on them.

Moving to the fourth level of the Taxonomy, there are two levels of the Organizing category: (a) *conceptualization of a value* and (b) *organization of a value system*.

Questions like "Is this what I understand you to say about that book . . . (interpret the reader's previous statement)?" and "Where do you suppose you first got interested in that kind of story?" aid the student in *conceptualizing a value*. In the first instance the student is given a chance to see what he has said and thus conceptualize more objectively the meaning of his utterance. In the second question, the student is asked to search his present conceptual structure to see if his statement fits into a pattern that is developing in his reading habits.

The teacher is helping the learner *organize his values* by asking, "What's really good about this book (or story) which makes it stand out from the other possibilities?" or "Is what you say consistent with what you said earlier?" The first clarifying response in essence asks the student to fit his choice in with his organized set of beliefs. The second is testing consistency in the student's organized set of values.

Again, these questions do not necessarily relate directly to reading, but they may grow out of a student's reading. The student needs an opportunity to respond personally to what he reads. The teacher ought to ask questions which will help the reader understand and evaluate his ideas, emotions, and values.

The top level on the internalization continuum, Characterization by a Value or Value Complex, is so intricate as to be almost mysterious. The

---

*Many of the clarifying questions quoted in this section were adapted from Louis E. Raths, *et al.*, *Values in Teaching*. The attempt to classify Raths' questions into categories of Krathwohl's Taxonomy is the responsibility of the author. Neither Raths nor Krathwohl have indicated that such a possibility exists, or that the author's attempt is valid.

Characterization category can best be described by quoting from the Taxonomy:

> At this level of internalization the values already have a place in the individuals' value hierarchy, are organized into some kind of internally consistent system, have controlled the behavior of the individual for a sufficient time that he has adapted to behaving this way; and an evocation of the behavior no longer arouses emotion or affect except when the individual is threatened or challenged (2).

The two levels of Characterization are (a) *generalized set*, and (b) *characterization*. The *generalized set* gives an internal consistency to the system of attitudes and values at any particular moment. Such questions as "Have you felt this way about reading for some time?" and "Will you read this author again?" help the student to evaluate his set. The prior response asks him to reflect on the durability of his feelings, while the latter helps him to see the pattern that has developed in his behavior.

Characterization, the highest level of the internalization continuum, is the totality of what a person is and what he is becoming. The master configuration of his generalized set of values and how the individual relates these to the larger world represent his character. As stated in the taxonomy,

> The great humanitarian figures of history—Socrates, Christ, Lincoln, Ghandi, Einstein—have achieved the characterization we refer to at this level. Each is universally held in high esteem precisely because his philosophy of life characterizes and pervades all of his behavior (2).

It is doubtful whether any questions or any way of evaluating behavior can be offered at this level. However, one can guide a student in developing other affective behaviors. At this level it is felt that the individual is independent; the valuing process is completely internalized; and the individual's own internal mechanism for processing, ordering, and selecting what he values takes over. The *characterization set* can be affected by influencing the learner at other affective levels, but whether or not he is led to restructure his character is an internal matter. Questions recommended by Raths are likely to help a learner come closer to realizing his transactive character and may lead one to develop a consistent value pattern. The clarifying response strategy appears to offer greater potential than any other technique at the moment.

Teachers may use observations, charts, tables, questions, and tests to measure and evaluate a learner's affective behavior at the first three levels of the Affective Taxonomy: Receiving, Responding, and Valuing. Teachers may ask questions and construct tests to help learners clarify and evaluate their own values about reading and what they have read at the three higher levels of the Taxonomy: Valuing, Organizing, and Characterization.

Some external rewards are likely to be necessary in guiding affective growth at the levels of Receiving, Responding, and Valuing. A learner must become dependent on internal rewards as the clarifying response strategy is used to encourage development of affective behavior at the levels of Valuing, Organizing, and Characterization.

Conclusion

Teachers are generally doing a good job of teaching the cognitive reading skills. If teachers are given leadership and encouragement in developing the learners' affective behavior, they will do a good job there, too.

Researchers need to provide teachers and textbook writers with information about affective behavior and how it is learned.

Professors and supervisors need to provide rational and practical strategies for teaching and evaluating the student's affective behavior in reading.

If the teacher-student interactions and the teacher-made tests analyzed here are representative of reading evaluation in general (and there is no strong reason to suspect otherwise), it appears that little or nothing is being done which assesses or evaluates the feelings, emotions, or values the learner has about reading or derives from reading. This lack represents a severe imbalance in reading instruction. The lack of evaluation of affective behavior is likely the cause of the erosion of interest on the part of teachers in affective learning.

There is evidence on college campuses across the country of the behavior that manifests itself when learning is depersonalized. The new frontier in education and in reading instruction is in the affective realm. Inventing new alphabets and applying linguistic techniques to reading instruction may improve the learning of cognitive reading skills, but the impact on affective behavior is far from clear. (Some linguistic readers I have seen don't do much to get me personally involved in reading.) The major concerns facing our country today are affective in nature. They are problems that relate to man's emotive forces, his attitudes, feelings, and values. The importance of being able to read is undeniable. Is it any less important to value reading and to use reading to develop one's character?

REFERENCES

1. Guszak, Frank J. "A Study of Teacher Solicitation and Student Response Interaction About Reading Content in Selected Second, Fourth, and Sixth Grades," unpublished doctoral dissertation, University of Wisconsin, 1965.
2. Krathwohl, David R., Benjamin S. Bloom, and Bertram B. Masia. *Taxonomy of Educational Objectives: Handbook II: Affective Domain.* New York: David McKay Co., Inc., 1964.

3. Mann, John S. "Functions of Curriculum Research," *Educational Leadership*, *24* (October, 1966), p. 85.
4. Raths, Louis E., Merrill Harmin, and Sidney Simon. *Values and Teaching*. Columbus, Ohio: Charles E. Merrill Books, Inc., 1966.
5. Robinson, Helen M., and others. *More Roads To Follow*. Chicago: Scott, Foresman, and Company, 1964.
6. Russell, David H., and others. *Finding New Friends*. Boston: Ginn and Company, 1964.

CURRENT TITLES IN THE PERSPECTIVES IN READING SERIES:

1. *College-Adult Reading Instruction*
2. *Reading Instruction in Secondary Schools*
3. *Children, Books and Reading*
4. *Developing Study Skills in Secondary Schools*
5. *First Grade Reading Programs*
6. *Corrective Reading in the High School Classroom*
7. *Corrective Reading in the Elementary Classroom*
8. *The Evaluation of Children's Reading Achievement*

NEW PRICES

Members **3.00**
Nonmembers 3.50

Copies are available for $2.50 each.
Send checks, payable to IRA, to:

INTERNATIONAL READING ASSOCIATION

P.O. Box 695　•　Newark, Delaware 19711